THE CURRENT ERA

Evaluating Nine Years of Governance and Controversies

VIGILANT

NewDelhi • London

BLUEROSE PUBLISHERS
India | U.K.

Copyright © Vigilant 2024

All rights reserved by author. No part of this publication may be reproduced, stored in a retrieval system or transmitted in any form or by any means, electronic, mechanical, photocopying, recording or otherwise, without the prior permission of the author. Although every precaution has been taken to verify the accuracy of the information contained herein, the publisher assumes no responsibility for any errors or omissions. No liability is assumed for damages that may result from the use of information contained within.

BlueRose Publishers takes no responsibility for any damages, losses, or liabilities that may arise from the use or misuse of the information, products, or services provided in this publication.

For permissions requests or inquiries regarding this publication, please contact:

BLUEROSE PUBLISHERS
www.BlueRoseONE.com
info@bluerosepublishers.com
+91 8882 898 898
+4407342408967

ISBN: 978-93-5819-548-4

Cover design: Shivam
Typesetting: Namrata Saini

First Edition: February 2024

Disclaimer

This book is a work of political commentary and analysis, intended to provide perspectives and insights on various political issues. The views expressed within these pages are those of the author and do not necessarily reflect the opinions of any specific political party, organisation, or individual.

The information presented in this book is based on the author's research, personal experiences, and understanding of the subject matter at the time of writing. Political landscapes are dynamic, and circumstances may change, leading to shifts in opinions and policies. Readers are encouraged to verify the information and consult additional sources for a comprehensive understanding of the issues discussed.

The author strives to maintain accuracy and objectivity, but it is important to acknowledge that political analysis involves interpretation and may be influenced by personal perspectives. Readers are encouraged to engage critically with the content, consider multiple viewpoints, and form their own informed opinions.

This book is not intended to provide legal, financial, or professional advice. Readers seeking such advice should consult appropriate professionals in the relevant fields.

The author and publisher disclaim any liability for any loss, harm, or damage arising directly or indirectly from the use or application of any information presented in this book. The content is for informational purposes only and is not a substitute for independent research or professional advice.

Readers should be aware that political discussions can evoke strong emotions and diverse opinions. The author encourages respectful and open dialogue, recognising the value of diverse perspectives in fostering a better understanding of complex political issues.

By reading this book, the reader acknowledges and agrees to the terms of this disclaimer.

Foreword

Reflecting on the drapery of governance and its myriad facades over nearly a decade is a noteworthy undertaking, one that offers an exclusive vantage point to evaluate the trajectory of a country's progress. "The Current Era: Evaluating 9 Years of Governance" (Indian context) compresses this journey—a chronicle steeped in the spirit of India's progression through the lens of governance.

India, a nation as assorted as it is vast, has circumnavigated a remarkable course over these years—a period categorized by transformative policies, socio-economic shifts, global arrangements, and internal recalibrations. Within these dynamic years, the drapery of governance has been intertwined with threads of innovation, challenges, reforms, and pliability.

This book stands as a testament to the penetration of analysis and thought-provoking exploration that pervades the pages within. It probes into the union of political narratives, policy applications, societal variations, and economic strategies that have molded India's contemporary scene. It does not purely chronicle events; rather, it seeks to decrypt the undercurrents that have defined this pivotal era.

As we examine the intricate interplay between governance and the ambitions of a billion people, this book is not just an examination of strategies and their impact; it is a reflection on the aspirations, dreams, and authenticities of every Indian. It encapsulates stories of suppleness, aspirations for a better tomorrow, and the unceasing pursuit of advancement that defines the Indian spirit.

The author, through his nuanced standpoints and meticulous research, has fashioned a narrative that invites reflection, contemplation, and dissertation. His insights encapsulate the intricacies and nuances of governance in a rapidly fluctuating world, offering a roadmap for future endeavors and disputes.

"The Current Era" is not just an assessment; it is a bidding—an invitation to engage, to question, to deliberate, and to envisage a future that aligns with the cooperative aspirations of a nation on the cusp of better transformations.

May this book serve as a scope, guiding us through the labyrinth of ascendency, illuminating the pathways we have treaded and those that lie forward.

Dr. Mariya H. Nad.
Member- Board of Directors
London Study Group, United Kingdom

Preface to "The Current Era: Evaluating Nine Years of Governance and Controversies"

I, as a secular democrat with firm faith in freedom of speech and expression as enshrined in our Indian Constitution, always wanted to serve the nation, cutting across barriers based on caste, creed, sex, colour, religion, or ethnicity to provide welfare and mitigate the skewed income distribution that exists even now after 75 years of independence. When India became independent, there were formidable challenges in making the people feel that our government and our constitution were the custodians of the hopes and aspirations of millions of people. Our forefathers gave a way to modern living where there was no scope for any discrimination in job and education opportunities. The government facilitated a base of agriculture and industry to provide job opportunities. Immediately after our constitution was adopted in 1950, there was a general election in 1951, which was the test of democracy that took its roots for years to come. We have got 17 Lok Sabha elections, and the forthcoming one is 18th in 2024. The Planning Commission was established in 1950, and thereafter, five-year plans started functioning in 1951 with the core objectives of growth and social justice. Infra-structural development started in order to make India develop from the backwardness of poverty and unemployment. The first three five-year plans laid more stress on agricultural investment than industrial development. This led to self-sufficiency in food production in the late sixties and early seventies, and finally the end of PL-480 programmes for food grains as part of US Policy 'Food for Peace.' But self-sufficiency in food production of grains did not mean food security among people, as the people had poor purchasing power and income distribution was much skewed. In order to speed up the development programmes, quality education in primary, secondary, and higher education started. The foundation of highly skilled technical education was laid with the opening of IITs in Kharagpur, Mumbai, Madras, Kanpur, and Delhi. Many universities at the central and state levels were opened to make higher education contribute to the country's development. The foundation of the iron and steel industries was laid with foreign collaboration in India in the 1950s and 1960s. The iron and steel industries in Bhilai and Bokaro were established in 1955 and 1964 with Russian collaboration. The Rourkela Steel Plant was established in 1959 with German collaboration. Durgapur Steel Plant was established in 1959 with UK collaboration. It was because of Nehru's vision to lay the infrastructure for the rapid industrialization of India that the foundation of heavy industries in India was laid. TISCO was already in the private sector to support the infrastructural development in India. A concept of the mixed economy had already come into being to provide social justice without monopolizing industries in favour of a select few. There was a rise in the propensity to save and the propensity to invest in productive channels, resulting in the creation of jobs. Banks were nationalized to involve them in the growth of national income by financing investments in the production process. The confidence of people in banks increased. Welfare measures were taken to check poverty and strike a balance between the rural and urban sectors by introducing MNREGA. Our economy was liberalized to give scope for reforms in the economy and raise foreign exchange. Thus, all-round development in terms of social justice, employment, and growth took place in India. This continued until 2014. Between 1947 and 2014, there were some changes in governance at the centre, but their impacts have not been such as reversing the development process and letting down the democratic system of governance. But with the BJP coming into power, led by Modi as PM of India, I found a complete reversal of the development process in India. In light of what I have witnessed in the development path of India during the last 75 years, I find the current era most disturbing when there is a flagrant violation of the rules of law. It was very shocking to see that the BJP government, which was formed with a thumping majority, was itself trying to subvert democratic processes. The other federal or balancing institutions have lost their independent role and have become subservient to the executives. Many socio-political and economic events that emerged proved that there was a backsliding of democracy. I found freedom of speech and expression under check for those who made silent protests against the government. They were put in jail. Many are still languishing in prison houses on one pretext or another. There have also been cases where the judiciary is under siege. The three pillars of the legislature, executive, and judiciary, which act independently and have leverage over one another, are now under attack. There is incitement to communal riots, there are human rights violations, and the federal institutions are unable to play their roles as guiding forces to uphold the constitution. I very well agree with what Christophe Jaffrelot compares to Modi's India as 'a riveting account of how a popularly elected leader has steered the world's largest democracy towards authoritarianism and intolerance (Jafferlot, 2021).'

The BJP and its think tank, the RSS, are incessantly working together to subvert the democratic process. Our constitution has been under attack, as according to them, there is nothing indigenous in it. As custodians of the hopes and aspirations of billions of people, the government should have acted proactively to check the communal riots and safeguard the common people without the law and order falling into the hands of hooligans, rather than becoming mute spectators to such unlawful happenings. Never before was our society divided on caste, creed, sex, ethnicity, or religious basis for the polarization of votes to gain power.

It is against this background that I have garnered the courage to write this book under the pen name "vigilant." As the book's blurb says, "The Current Era: Evaluating Nine Years of Governance and Controversies." There are eleven chapters, viz. (i) "From Hope to Disillusionment: Unfulfilled Expectations from the Current Government;" (ii) "Our constitution is under threat;" (iii) "The principle of Federalism is at stake;" (iv) "Erosion of Democratically Established Institutions;" (v) "Human Rights Violation;" (vi) "Utter disregard for farmers' problems;" (vii) "Economic Policy Framework from Welfare to Crony Capitalism;" (viii) "Abetment to Communal Riots;" (ix) "Lack of Welfare Measures, Unemployment, and Poverty;" (x) "Curtailment of the Power of the Judiciary;" and (xi) "Climate Change and its Adaptation" that justify the main theme of the book. These chapters have been very well documented and supported by relevant references. As these chapters unfold, the reader will find a critical account of the governance, controversies, and challenges that our country is facing after the ensuing Modi regime. As you become more critical, you will find that Modi and his government are failing in their responsibility to serve India. How enthusiastic were we to vote in the belief that Modi would change the fate of India from poverty to growth in income and employment? He had promised to check poverty and end exploitation. He had promised to check black money in India and bring black money deposited in foreign banks. In this connection, he promised to deposit a sum of ₹15 lakhs each into the accounts of every citizen of India. He also ensured an employment generation of 20 million each year. Naturally, the BJP government, which was formed on lofty goals led by Mr. Narendra Modi, was never to be successful on various parameters as promised to the people. During the last nine years, different controversies have erupted referring to the structure of the balance of powers among the executive, legislature, and judiciary, the issue of protection of our constitution concerning the right to freedom of speech and expression, excitation to communal tensions, flaring up of social tensions based on caste, inter-religious differences, and erosion of democratically established autonomous institutions. In many instances, Modi has lowered the dignity of the Prime Minister when he mimics the leaders of opposing parties. Unlike Bajpayee, the former PM of the BJP, who believed in the Rajya Dharma of equality of states and non-polarization of votes on caste, sex, and religion, Modi is involved in the polarization of votes and discriminates against people for votes. This has led to social tensions among different communities. Where Bajpayee believed in social harmony, Modi believed in social inequality.

All former PMs had their vision of developing the nation based on our constitution, which Modi lacks. He does not have regard for any dissent about his policies.

We have never seen any press conferences he has taken, unlike the erstwhile PMs. His vision is to establish 'Hindu Rashtra' where the majority population has supremacy and the minorities have second-hand citizenship. Jawahar Lal Nehru speaks of the rich heritage of India in his "Discovery of India." But he always emphasized that we cannot live in the past. He believed in a looking, modern, and tolerant nation fostering peace and cooperation. He was extremely nationalistic, but he believed that this nationalism did not degenerate into a narrow variety that ultimately did more harm than good. Perhaps the BJP's nationalism in establishing a 'Hindu Rashtra' will do more harm than good to our nation. This is now reflected in the nine years of misrule in India. Every day, we come across discrimination against people based on caste, creed, sex, colour, religion, and ethnicity, which goes against the spirit of nationalism.

To conclude, we can state that considering the vast diversities unparalleled in the world, it is very difficult to ensure justice, fraternity, and equality for all people. Despite the assertion of protection of life and personal liberty in our constitution, which is available to every person and foreigner alike, we find that during Modi's regime from 2014 to 2019 and again in the post-2019 period, instead of minimizing the violations of human rights, the cases have gotten accentuated, especially after 2019. As the trend shows, we are moving towards an authoritarian regime. Our democracy is backsliding. It is very shameful. We must rise above narrow parochialism and identify ourselves as the most secular democracy in the world.

Some political scientists warn of the backsliding of democracy in India. For example, since 2019, the Sweden-based Varieties of Democracies project has classified India as "an electoral autocracy"; in 2023, it called India "one of the worst autocracies in the last 10 years" (Ibid.). The France-based Rights without Borders' (RSF) 2023 Press Freedom Index ranks India 161st of 180 countries, down from 150th in 2022. RSF says that there is a continuing downward trend.

A welfare-oriented government would like to lower the crime rate to establish peace by not discriminating against existing law and order. The principle of maximum social advantage works on minimizing taxation and, in return, providing welfare in terms of an increase in amenities, an increase in employment generation, and investment in public utility services like roads, schools, transport, and communication for more productivity. But during the Modi regime, there was more taxation, and welfare returns were much lower. Only a few business enterprises are the beneficiaries of the uneven income distribution policy of the government. His policy of digitization and ease of administration has only benefited crony capitalists. In the US, there is an anti-trust law that checks the monopoly or group interest-profit motive attitude of capitalists (Chen, May 2, 2022). This law encourages fair competition among entrepreneurs for the maximization of welfare. The present regime in India is unlike the US anti-trust law, where the government has been giving all industries to a select few capitalists. This is against the economic empowerment and social inclusion that our constitution guarantees. This is also very much like an infringement on the human rights of the people.

The book is not only a study of governance and controversies but also of the challenges India is facing to re-establish itself as a sovereign, secular, socialist, and democratic republic. As the author has discussed, there has been a radical shift in policy from welfare to crony capitalism. Our economy has moved into oligopoly as most of the prominent PSUs are in the grip of a select few entrepreneurs, leading to a hike in the prices of public utility services. Due to the failure of the digitization programme, most MNREGA wagers have been deprived of their wages. Promising to start ten universities in the public sector and ten in the private sector on par with the best universities in the world is nowhere in the picture. Did we get any benefit from scrapping the Planning Commission and substituting it with the NITI Ayog? The economy will flourish when demand is created by investing in agriculture and developing infrastructural facilities. On the development parameter, the BJP government has failed, but on the sidelines of other parameters, as discussed in different chapters, the BJP has succeeded in its silent programmes of divisive politics, dividing the people on caste, creed, ethnicity, and religious basis. It has also succeeded in polarizing votes on its Hindutva agenda, as propounded by the RSS. Naturally, nine years of BJP governance have led to the backsliding of democracy by the declaration of a "Hindu Rashtra," which is a direct threat to our constitution, by diluting federalism which is the soul of democracy, by eroding democratically established institutions, by not taking strict actions against human rights violations, by the police administration being neutral to the abetment of communal riots, by executives having control over the judiciary, by the government having disregard for farmers' problems, and a shift away from the welfare state to oligopoly, where there are a select few having control over production functions. This might ultimately lead to the revival of a new form of colonial regime.

Vigilant

Editor's Review

The writing style in the passage under review is marked by a potent and critical tone, reflecting a profound sense of disillusionment and disappointment with the current government, particularly Prime Minister Narendra Modi's leadership. The author employs a strategic blend of formal language, factual information, and subjective opinions to articulate their perspective on the government's performance over the past nine years.

One notable feature is the extensive use of rhetorical devices, a tool effectively wielded to emphasise the perceived shortcomings of the government. Phrases such as "nine years of misrule" and "unfulfilled expectations" are recurrent, creating a palpable sense of disappointment and frustration. This deliberate use of repetition serves to underscore the author's discontent and contributes to the overall persuasive impact of the passage. The author also resorts to historical references, drawing comparisons with past leaders like Atal Bihari Vajpayee, strategically employed to underscore their points and draw a compelling contrast with Modi's approach.

The structure of the passage is commendably organised, featuring a clear delineation of specific instances and issues contributing to the author's overarching argument. It opens with a retrospective view of Modi's promises during his election campaign, outlining the expectations set by the government. Subsequently, the author adeptly delves into specific incidents and controversies, providing detailed examples to substantiate their critical assessment. This structured approach not only enhances the readability of the passage but also allows for a systematic presentation of the author's critique.

The passage maintains a fine balance between formal and informal language, rendering it accessible to a broad audience. While navigating through the intricacies of political and constitutional matters, the author seamlessly incorporates colloquial expressions and direct criticisms, imbuing the narrative with a personal touch. Anecdotes, such as the incident involving Alapan Bandopadhyay, are strategically employed to humanise the discourse, bringing attention to the perceived arbitrary actions of the government and invoking a sense of relatability among readers.

A notable strength of the passage lies in the consistent effort to provide evidence and examples to fortify the author's claims, thereby enhancing the credibility of the critique. The text astutely draws attention to issues pertaining to democracy, governance, and the alleged erosion of democratic principles. The arguments put forth by the author are underpinned by a clear political perspective, and the language chosen consistently aligns with the critical stance adopted throughout the passage.

Shifting focus to the broader context, the writing effectively addresses historical nuances, tracing India's journey from a dominion state to a federal republic. The mention of princely states and the strategic use of military force to integrate them into the Union of India adds a valuable historical perspective to the discussion. This contextualization serves to enrich the reader's understanding of the complexities inherent in India's federal structure.

As the passage seamlessly transitions to contemporary issues, it sheds light on the period from 2014 to 2023, homing in on the conflict between the Delhi government and the Centre, particularly the contentious role of the Lieutenant Governor. The author navigates this complex terrain with clarity, supporting their assertions with references to specific legal judgments. The inclusion of the S. R. Bommai case further fortifies the legal weight of the argument, providing a comprehensive backdrop to the challenges faced by federalism in India.

While the author successfully articulates their points, a constructive critique could suggest occasional brevity to enhance readability. Some sentences tend to be lengthy and intricate, and breaking them down could improve the overall flow, ensuring that the reader remains engaged without feeling overwhelmed by the density of the content.

In conclusion, the writing style in this passage is commendable for its comprehensive, analytical approach and its deep understanding of the subject matter. The author adeptly combines historical context, legal perspectives, and contemporary events to present a nuanced analysis of the challenges to federalism in India. The strategic use of rhetorical devices, balanced tone, and evidence-based arguments contribute to the overall effectiveness of the passage, making it a compelling critique of the government's handling of federalism in India.

Contents

From Hope to Disillusionment: Unfulfilled Expectations from the Current Government 1

Our Constitution is under Threat 10

The Principle of Federalism is at Stake 20

Erosion of Democratically Established Institutions 29

Human Rights Violations 41

Utter Disregard for Farmers' Problems 54

Economic Policy Framework from Welfare to Crony Capitalism 64

Abetment to Communal Riots 69

Lack of Welfare Measures, Unemployment, and Poverty 76

Curtailment of Power of Judiciary 88

Climate Change and Its Adaptation 96

References 107

From Hope to Disillusionment: Unfulfilled Expectations from the Current Government

Today is the 26th of May when Narendra Damodar Bhai Modi was sworn in as the Prime Minister of India in 2014. Nine years have passed since he took reign as the Prime Minister. I, as a citizen of India liked Modi much as he appeared to represent a common man full of promises to serve the people with honesty and free from any biases. We were very much enthusiastic to vote in the belief that Modi would change the fate of India from poverty to growth of income and employment. He would be the custodian of the hopes and aspirations of billions of people. He would safeguard our constitution. He would protect the right to freedom of speech and expression. He would build up democratic institutions and strengthen them to give social justice to all irrespective of caste, creed, sex, colour or religion. He had promised to check poverty and end exploitation. He had promised to check black money in India and bring black money deposited in foreign banks. In this connection, he promised to deposit a sum of ₹15 lakhs each into the accounts of each and every citizen of India. He also ensured employment generation of 20 million each year. According to him, the past sixty years of rule of his adversary was the rule of exploitation, looting and selling the nation. Once voted to power, he would ensure removal of poverty, and unemployment, and safeguard the rights of each and every individual of this nation. The erstwhile government which had legacy of apparent corruption charges and the anti-incumbency effect made people walk away against the Congress Party and they voted against it. Although the erstwhile government had a comparative good economic performance which unfortunately did not percolate to the common man (Sharma, 2019), it could not ensure a welfare state to the people. Naturally, the BJP government which was formed on lofty goals led by Mr. Narendra Modi was never to be successful on various parameters as promised to the people. Modi had cajoled people not to help the nation but to help him and a coterie of people who supported him to win the election.

Of nine years of misrule by the BJP government led by Modi you can just evaluate his governance by his different laws which are detrimental to the national interest. Different controversies that have erupted refer to the structure of the balance of powers among the executive, the legislature and judiciary, the issue of protection of our constitution with regard to right to freedom of speech and expression, excitation to communal tensions, flaring up of social tensions based on caste, inter-religious differences, and erosion of democratically established autonomous institutions.

In the most recent controversy, there was a warrant from the PMO to Alapan Bandopadhyay, the Chief Secretary of West Bengal who was to retire on 31st May 2021, but his service was extended for another three months during Covid Pandemic after the request of Mamta Banerjee, the Chief Minister of West Bengal. The Centre wanted the CS to report to the PMO on the first of June. The letter appeared very vindictive and arbitrary by the PMO as Alapan Bandopadhyay was to retire on 31st May itself, and he was given an extension to fight against the pandemic in West Bengal. Actually, Ms.

Mamta Banerjee for some pre-assigned work could not attend a meeting proposed to be held between the CM and PM in connection with the assessment of relief to be given to West Bengal against the Cyclone Yaas damages to lives and livelihoods.

Mamta had sought permission to be excused from the meeting with the Prime Minister. As the Chief Secretary to the Chief Minister, Alapan had no alternative but to accompany the CM. Consequently, Alapan Bandopadhyay was unable to attend the meeting. However, prior to requesting leave, the CS had already provided the PM with the necessary proposal details. Unfortunately, the PMO perceived the CS's actions as a breach of discipline and ordered him to report to the PMO on June 1, 2021.

He was also given show cause notice of his dereliction of duty. Such kind of action on the part of the PMO is very demoralizing and it speaks of high-handed arbitrariness in administering the All India Services. Such action was again regarded as very vindictive and this goes against the healthy practice of liaison between the PMO and the state secretariat. Meanwhile, Alapan Bandopadhyay resigned an extension letter and took his retirement on 31st May only. Subsequently, Mamta Banerjee appointed Alapan Bandopadhyay as an advisor to her cabinet. Ultimately, the case will be decided by the court in due course of time. But such an instance speaks of unhealthy relations between the Centre and state. Here, the PMO should rise against such narrow and parochial consideration and must take a prudent approach lest the relation between the Centre and State suffers. There are many such instances when you would feel that the subordinate offices are maltreated. The governments of opposition parties regularly suffer in maintaining a healthy relationship with the Centre. You would always find some discrimination on the part of the Centre in giving aids to the states.

Prior to assuming office as Prime Minister in 2014, we have heard him deliver speeches at public rallies on various occasions. Each time he spoke, his sincerity in promising to address issues such as unemployment, poverty alleviation, and agricultural concerns was evident. He passionately discussed the challenges of rising prices and the devaluation of the rupee, likening the situation to being in the Intensive Care Unit (ICU) during the previous UPA regime. Additionally, he criticized the former government for its perceived shortcomings in defense preparedness.

But once he became the Prime Minister, he forgot everything. Most of his promises are unfulfilled; they are mere gimmicks. He took everything to his advantage and befooled people. The PM being at the head of a federal country like ours, he should take extra care in developing an ideal federal relation with the states irrespective of whether the ruling party of the states are in opposing or not.

In many instances, Modi has lowered the dignity of the Prime Minister when he does mimicry of leaders of opposing parties. Unlike Bajpayee, the former PM of BJP who believed in Rajya Dharma of equality of states and non-polarization of votes on caste, sex, and religion, Modi involves in polarization of votes and discriminates against people for votes. This has led to social tensions among different communities. Where Bajpayee believed in social harmony, Modi believes in social inequality.

During his entire career as Prime Minister, Modi never took questions from the press on policy decisions. He lacks confidence as he gives his monologues only. It reflects a dictatorial attitude toward the opposition and press. In a nutshell, we can say he has become an autocrat and his behaviour is unlike that of PM who should be above the narrow parochialism in safeguarding the interests of people.

In the following paragraph, we give certain parameters of being a good premier. Whether Modi has any of such parameters that the former Prime Ministers have followed when he has risen from a common man to the status of CM of Gujarat, and finally to the status of Prime Minister of India. How former PMs have behaved in comparative situations? They have had very rich tradition of public life and public address. Possibly they were far superior on different traits which are essentially required to be the PM of any nation. They maintained the gravity of the Prime Minister by being impartial, by acting as custodians of the hopes and aspirations of billions of people. The different traits among others are (i) integrity (ii) ability to delegate (iii) communication (iv) self-awareness (v) gratitude (vi) learning ability (vii) influence (viii) empathy (ix) courage, and (x) respect (Centre for Creative Leadership, Greensboro, NC27410, USA). To me, these traits are essentially required for quality leadership. But in public life when you become at the helms, you should see that you use these traits for the welfare of the people, for raising the status of the country among the comity of nations, and for unflinching faith to serve the nation on the path of employment generation, income generation, checking the iniquitous distribution of income existing between the rich and poor, and all-round development of growth and development. It also means to treat each people equally without any discrimination based on caste, creed, sex, colour or religion. Here, one can cite former PM Bajpayee who believed in 'Raj Dharma' in his address to parliament in 2004 (Bajpayee Address to seek vote of Confidence in 2004).

Raj Dharma, as per his understanding, called for impartial policy decisions in line with our constitution. It was due to Bajpayee's sincere efforts that the BJP witnessed significant growth, progressing from a mere 2 seats in Parliament in 1984 to forming a government at the Centre for the first time in 1996. His commitment to Raj Dharma, coupled with the ideology of Hindutva, pseudo-secularism, and inclusive outreach to the Muslim community, contributed to the party's success, garnering 182 seats in 1999. Bajpayee's leadership also facilitated alliances with other parties, leading to the BJP government's full-term tenure until 2004, with a combined strength of 270. Following Bajpayee's exit from active politics, there was a leadership vacuum in the BJP until Modi emerged as the party's leader in 2014. However, in his new role, Modi deviated from Raj Dharma and utilized the Hindutva ideology to polarize Hindu votes.

All former PMs had their vision of developing the nation on the basis of our constitution which Modi lacks. He does not have regard to any dissent on his policies. We have never seen any press conference he has taken unlike the erstwhile PMs. His vision is of establishing 'Hindu Rashtra' where the majority population has the supremacy and the minorities would have second hand citizenship. Jawahar Lal Nehru speaks of rich heritage of India in his "Discovery of India." But he always emphasized that we cannot live in the past. He believed in forward looking, modern and tolerant nation fostering peace and cooperation. He was extremely nationalistic, but he believed that this nationalism does not degenerate into a narrow variety which ultimately does more harm than good. Perhaps BJP's nationalism of establishing a Hindu Rashtra will do more harm than good to our nation. This is now reflected during the nine years of misrule in India. Every day we come across discrimination of people based on caste, creed, sex, colour, religion, and ethnicity which go against the spirit of nationalism. Modi does not even honour Lok Sabha as is seldom found in participation in debates. Nehru regularly used to listen to the members of parliament whether of ruling or of opposition. Nehru was well educated which we do not find in Modi. A person as great as PM must be well read and he should be above narrow parochialism which is the regular feature of Modi in his monologues and utterances in public rallies. Public addresses were never as mean as done by Modi in criticizing his opponents. His recent address to Ms. Mamta Banerjee as "Didi- O- Didi" has surpassed the lowest of low addresses in public rallies. Such an unscrupulous remark does not behove the post of Prime Minister.

In an interview with a private TV channel (which he has never given to any TV channel, nor has he faced any press conference) he said that he was for the poor and his whole life was devoted to the welfare of poor people. But when Modi became the PM we hardly find anything in support of the poor people. Rather, he has worked for the capitalists and corporate tycoons in helping them grow crony capitalism.

Every year on 25th June, the BJP celebrates this day as "black day" for "Indian Democracy" as it was on this day Mrs. Gandhi had declared State of emergency on 25th June 1975 that continued for 21 months until 21st March 1977. Mr. Modi on this day tweeted that his all-party workers should hold video conferencing for condemning the Congress regime for an emergency. But Mr. Modi appears to be a hypocrite as in his nine years of rule; there is an undeclared emergency where things are unparalleled. There are more violations of human rights and freedom without any compunction. There are rapes of girls and many journalists are under detention under NSA. There is an environment of fear and tyranny among a section of honest citizens. The people cannot speak against the government policy. The morale of unlawful elements is high as they have the support of the government. There are instances when a journalist and an activist of Manipur were put in jail by the district magistrate for a heinous crime of saying on Facebook that 'corona cannot be cured by cow dung and cow urine but by science." It is shameful that the Modi government takes no action on such issues. Modi lets it continues as this helps him divide the people which his government would use for polarization of votes.

Before entering the parliament he prostrated himself before the parliament pretending to be the most honest follower of the Indian constitution. But now in practice, we find him failing in protecting the basic framework of our constitution. There have been more violations of the right to freedom of speech and expression during his regime than during the governments of yester years.

The PM has abundant power to appoint the staff of PMO as per his choice crossing the state boundaries and IAS rules. Modi has imported his staff from his home state Gujarat and spread them to the different states for his support. Most of the IAS officers who are working in critical positions hail from Gujarat only. Such an attitude leads to a kind of discrimination against other genuine officers. This has led to humiliation among other IAS officers who are from different cadres. Naturally, the PMO obeys to his dictates ignoring the responsibility for which they have been appointed.

We give below the issues on which Modi has either ignored or completely failed or abused the law to take advantage in his own favour. Abraham Lincoln said,

"Nearly all men can stand adversity, but if you want to test a man's character, give him power" (Lincoln, Abraham, 16th US President, 1809-1865). He led the nation through the American Civil War, the country's greatest moral, cultural, constitutional and political crisis. But Modi changed his character once he became Prime Minister of India. Unlike other PMs of India, he became power-hungry and became indifferent to the hopes and aspirations of billions of the population. Like a Machiavellian (Niccolo Machiavelli 1513), Modi appears to be sneaky, cunning, and lacking a moral code. He believes in opportunistic ways of manipulating the population of this country. He also appears to have a narcissistic personality as he has an inflated sense of self-importance.

******

Our Constitution is under Threat

By default, the RSS which is the think tank of the BJP believes in the creation of 'Hindu Rashtra'. Mr. Modi being a follower of the RSS has never denied this objective which is in direct conflict with the secular state as enshrined in the preamble of our constitution. Once we go for 'Hindutva' which craves for 'Hindu Nationalism' what comes out is a creation of a non-secular state in which the minorities would be treated as second category citizens. This concept took its genesis in factions of the Indian National Congress in the first half of the 20th Century which continued to be identified with "Hindu Politics" and ideas of a Hindu nation (Wikipedia, 2022). Since Hindu society is dependent on caste hierarchy, there is ample scope for exploitation and hence division of society on caste lines. Pundit Jawaharlal Nehru who was the first PM and had devoted his entire life in the freedom struggle, knew that our old rich tradition must give way to the modern scientific thinking of a tolerant- nation. In this tolerant nation, all people irrespective of caste, colour, religion or ethnicity would foster peace and cooperation to make India a truly secular nation. Our constitution which is the embodiment of the hopes and aspirations of all living beings in India, encompasses all sections of society. To Nehru, each individual is treated as a community. Our constitution makers did their best to provide us a constitutional framework where there is equality of every individual, and there are no discriminations in jobs and opportunities. Its basic features of sovereignty, democracy, secularism, socialism, and republic stand sacrosanct. Since the establishment of RSS, there has been a constant effort to address their main agenda of creating "Hindu Rashtra," and accordingly, the BJP has been inspired to follow their preaching. Though the two units are disjoint, and they claim to be independent of each other; but the RSS prepares the ground of organisational set up of BJP in policy formulations which have bearing on the day to day administration of the country. Those who are associated with the RSS are normally recommended to participate in the political activities of the BJP. Mr. Atal Bihari Bajpayee and Mr. Narendra Modi are the products of the RSS only. Bajpayee was an earnest statesman who believed in 'Rajya dharma'. At many occasions, Bajpayee was at variance with the RSS on their original agenda of formation of "Hindu Rashtra". He had a strong belief in the Indian constitution. His heart was too magnanimous to discriminate any faith be it Hindu, Muslim, Sikh, Jain or Christian. For India to be vibrant and most liveable in the world, we must adhere to the 'universal declaration of human rights' of the UN (UN, 1948). At this juncture, the Communists, the Muslims, and Christians are anathema to the RSS, and hence they openly discriminate. This is in direct conflict with our constitution.

The RSS is opposed to our constitution and our national flag. Our constitution guarantees the fundamental right to propagate religion by Article 25. But, the VHP (Vishwa Hindu Parishad) its outfit rejects the constitution. It is not a secret that its political wing BJP has ever denied this rejection (Noorani, A G, 2019). The RSS rejects the national flag, and tricolour, and unfurls the saffron flag 'Bhagwa Dhwaj.' The RSS denounced the constitution on January 1, 1993, when they published a white paper. They are reported to have said that the Constitution has done more harm than the two hundred years of British rule. In its foreword, Swami Hirananda had written that "The constitution is contrary to India's culture, character, circumstances, situation, etc. It is foreign-oriented (Noorani, A G)." He is reported to have again said that only after nullifying the present constitution, do we have to think afresh of our economic policies, nature of administration, and character of national institutions. The RSS does not accept the present composite culture in which all religions flourish. They refuse to accept the Muslims, the Communists, and Christians in our culture.

After the demolition of the Babri Masjid (6 December 1992), the RSS took a calculated move on 25 December 1992 when Swami Muktananda called a press conference and exhorted the people to reject the constitution as anti-Hindu. He said that they had no faith in the laws of the nation, and "the sadhus are above the law of the land." He also stated that India's citizenship laws that deem all born in India as natural citizens, are deceptive. The then RSS de facto supreme Rajendra Singh (popularly called Rajju Bhaiya), the first non-Maharashtrian Sarsangchalak of the RSS in January 1993 wanted incorporation of "Bharat that is Hindustan" instead of "India that is Bharat" in the Indian constitution. A constitution that suits the ethos and genius of the country should be adopted in the future. Even M. M. Joshi, the then BJP President on 24th January 1993 had reiterated that "Westernized people unfamiliar with the culture and history of India are the creators of our constitution."

It is really shameful for the BJP to get inspiration from their philosopher guide, the RSS, to condemn our constitution, reject the tri-colour and deny the composite culture. It is more condemnable when they say that the constitution has done more harm than the rule of 200 years of Great Britain. Our constitution symbolises the hopes and aspirations of billions of people cutting across caste, creed, sex, religion and ethnic barriers. Our constitution really represents our ethos and genius. After its adoption on 26th January 1950, our constitution has moved forward on the development path. All challenging issues have been addressed, and it is most apt to suit the genius of people. The fundamental rights and directive principles of state policy are constantly tailored to mitigate any differences existing among our communities. How troublesome our freedom- struggle has been! As the demand of the RSS goes for a very sectarian Hindu Rashtra, it would lead to further division of our society, leading to a fascist system of autocracy. This would ultimately lead to slavery where a select few castes or communities would rule the whole nation. Our constitution makers were visionary enough to adopt separation of powers, and scientific temperament to enact laws for composite culture. The day on which a Hindu-Rashtra is created in which other faiths become subservient to the 'Hindutva', there would be the end of India or Bharata.

As the people are not educated, and less aware of their constitutional rights, they are easily cajoled by the RSS to have a narrow conservative outlook towards society; thereby they develop a fanatic attitude against certain communities.

Modi being the PM of our nation should have addressed the nation on these issues that hinder the growth of scientific temperament among the people! But there has not been any occasion when he directed his officials and party workers to refrain from such unlawful statements.

In recent times, Sadhvi Pragya Singh Thakur who is an MP from Bhopal on a BJP ticket considers Nathu Ram Godse who assassinated Mahatma Gandhi, as a patriot. This attracted criticism from all sections of society. Consequently, she was removed from the consultative parliamentary team on defence as well as from BJP Parliamentary Party meetings. The BJP should have removed her as an MP for calling Godse a patriot. Sadhvi Pragya was accused in the 2008 Malegaon blast where 10 people were killed and 82 more were injured. She was arrested on terror charges under the Unlawful Activities (Prevention) Act after her bike was found to be used in the bomb blast. Later in 2017, she was granted bail on health grounds and the NIA dropped some of the serious charges. Why was she given the BJP ticket to fight the 2019 Lok Sabha election when she is accused of unlawful activities? During the Covid-19 pandemic she was seen putting cow dung on her body with a claim that rubbing of cow-dung on body would protect the person from the corona. Its urine is also a medicine which if taken by the people would get protection from corona. Such orthodox things she has been practising with her followers, although she herself underwent Covid-19 treatment. Such practices thrust our people into backwardness. This practice should have been condemned by the RSS and BJP. A strict law should be enacted to check such hypocritical things which undermine the unity and progress of our country. The more such rituals are followed, the more shall there be divisions of society, and there would be more exploitations of downtrodden families. We wished Modi to come forward and address the nation on these issues. There should be an amendment in the People's Representation Act of 1950 to screen out such people who are too conservative to accept the scientific development of the country.

Veer Savarkar who is regarded by RSS as a freedom fighter from Maharashtra and who was alleged to have his hand in the assassination of Mahatma Gandhi has a false reputation. He was a coward who wrote a letter to the British Raj for pardoning him, and he promised to be the most obedient servant of the British Raj. He even got a pension for his livelihood from the British Raj. His letter written from the cellular jail of Andaman is in the public domain which anyone can see (Noorani A G, 2005). The BJP has never condemned Veer Savarkar who had anti-national activities. Modi too refrains from such condemnation. Naturally, the BJP and RSS have a nefarious role of dividing India, but they could not do as they had a very limited sphere of influence in pre-independence period. It is only in the post-independence era that such forces of anti-Hindu and anti-national activities have increased, and the present regime of Modi has given a boost to these forces. Logically, there is a real threat to our constitution.

Mindful of the fact that Veer Savarkar was born on 28th May 1883, Modi decided to inaugurate the newly constructed Parliament on this day in 2023. The way the parliament was inaugurated by Modi himself barring the President and Vice-President, it laid stress on executive power more than the constitutional head. This act is against the balance of separation of powers among the legislature, executive and judiciary. This is definitely like a nail at the beginning of the killing of democracy in India. It substantiates the beginning of the emergence of an authoritarian regime in India.

In the present era, Modi and his coterie want to assert that the parliament is supreme, and any decision that the parliament takes is beyond the purview of the judiciary. On this basis, they intend to subjugate the judiciary, and they want control of the judiciary by the parliament. They forget the supremacy of the constitution that asserts a balance of power among the executive, legislature and judiciary. The government has become autocratic as the opposition parties are not consulted in law-making bills. The BJP being the most resourceful party in the country, has tried to topple the State Governments by horse-trading. Even money bills have passed without the participation of the opposition in the parliament. As crony capitalism is at its peak in Modi's regime, we find undue favour to Adani who has special relations with Modi. The Hindenburg Report which had a catastrophic impact on the share market exposed the manipulated price of the stock exchange from January 23 to March 23 (Hindenburg, 2023). It showed how inflated user metrics and "frictionless fraud" facilitations enabled insiders to cash out over $ 1 billion. Rahul Gandhi, the congress MP in Parliament who has raised questions on Adani –Modi relationship has been cornered, and his speech is expunged. Instead of answering his questions, his voice is muted and at times the whole parliament is muted. Does it not show a fascist tendency not to listen to the voice of the opposition? There have been repeated requests of opposition to constitute a JPC (Joint Parliamentary Committee) and institute an enquiry into the corruption of Adani industries. But these demands have not been accepted by the ruling party. Earlier also the demands of the opposition to review the purchase of Dassault Rafale fighter air crafts by the supreme court became null and void as the government did not cooperate. In order to silence the voice of opposition, the government resorts to CBI, NIA and ED. Since the government formation of BJP in 2014, there are seldom cases of BJP lawmakers where CBI, NIA and ED have carried out raids. It is mostly the opposition parties where the raids have been carried out. The PMLA (Prevention of Money Laundering Act) was enacted in 2002, but implemented from July 1, 2005. Raids carried out by the ED from 2004 to 2022 saw a nearly 27-fold increase to 3010 as compared to 112 searches from 2004 to 2014 (India Times, 2022). This shows the government is interested in shutting the mouth of the opposition rather than preventing money laundering.

Recently most of retired civil servants have written to the President that there is constant effort by the government to put pressure on them to be loyal to the government. They have undergone pressure to act likewise lest they suffer. Sardar Patel had formed this steel frame 'Civil Services' to safeguard the Indian constitution, and the civil servants take a promise to act in the interest of our constitution without any fear or favour and without any discrimination based on divisive politics (The Wire, 2023). Thus, intimidating the civil servants on the part of the executive is like killing the soul of the constitution.

Democracy gets strengthened or becomes stronger when its federal institutions that are responsible for protecting the basic structure of Constitution become stronger. But once these federal institutions are intimidated to follow or be loyal to the centre, democracy starts dying out (Lewitski and Ziblatt, 2018). There would be no checks and balances. During the last nine years of governance, we observe that there are serious or constant efforts by the centre to crumble these institutions in letter and spirit so that the constitution could be altered to serve the autocratic government.

Democracies are always fragile, but they need to be protected. Our strong and largest democracy has stood the test of time because of a strong federal structure, and love for democracy by the middle class barring some aberration of the past of imposition of emergency and some resurgence of divisive politics like 'Hindutva', which is taking its roots in fanaticism.

How can we judge that democracy is strong? We can judge by the functioning of federal institutions in close coordination with the objective of Constitution. The people must have high moral of brotherhood cutting across the differences based upon equality, fraternity, and freedom of speech and expression. People must have quality education to contribute to development. All people must be educated and they must follow the law and order. The executive, legislature and judiciary must respect each other to make our life simple and without fear or favour. The government must also look for mitigating the income diversity existing between the rich and poor. The government must also explore avenues for employment generation. The government must also work in close coordination with the democratic institutions of the world. We must also follow the latest development parameters and make our students participate. Everyone must feel that there are enough opportunities, there is enough to share, and there is also enough to contribute to making our nation stronger than ever before. It does not matter whichever government comes, but once the parameters of democracy become strong we shall be an example for other developing countries to follow our model.

What is happening now- a-days is that there is religious fanaticism in the name of 'Hindutva' and constant efforts to establish ethnic democracy that would always have the tension of dominance of one tribe over another. Efforts to polarize the votes based on the majority of caste or tribe doctrine would lead us to revitalization of slavery again that happened in the past. If our laws are philanthropic, we would continue ourselves to be a strong democratic nation.

But the fact is during the last nine years of governance, there is a constant effort to dilute the constitution and make the federal institutions crumble to serve the sole objective of dividing the society for BJP rule.

******

The Principle of Federalism is at Stake

India is a union of states with a bias towards the Centre. It is 'quasi-federal' (Wheare, K C). It is between a unitary state and a federation. All states share power with the Centre. It is unlike the United States of America where all autonomous states joined together to form a federal government at the Centre. It is more federal than unitary in character. There is a division of power between the central government and the state governments. In addition to the US, there are Switzerland, Australia, and Canada which have a federal form of government. Thus, the salient feature of the federal government is to have dual governments at the Centre and at State levels. They have a separation of powers. They have a rigid and written constitution. They have supremacy of the constitution and they also have independence of judiciary. In tune with an idea to separate powers between the Centre and States, in India, there are the State List and the Union list of political issues. There is also a concurrent list where both the Centre and States share power. Since India was a dominion state of the UK, it took years to become independent. India had princely states which opposed their annexation to the formation of the Union of India. Hence, a strong military force was used to annex them into India. Naturally, with the demarcations of states, a unitary state was constituted. We have only one constitution of which all States and Union territories are part of India. Federalism is the soul of democracy. It is central to the resilience of India's democracy (Tillin, Louise. 2019). Democracy is strengthened if the Centre and the States follow the principles of federalism. Once the power gets concentrated in the Centre and the States have least to share from the Centre, anarchy develops. As a result, democracy is choked, development suffers, and welfare is at the whims of the autocratic regime at the Centre.

Although Indian federalism is intermediate between the complete autonomy of the States and unitary force at the Centre, but as our democracy evolved, the constitution also evolved to accommodate the changing needs of the people. The biggest challenge which Indian federalism faces is from the complexities and ambiguities generated within the resulting federal order. The Centre went under decentralization of power to suit the local needs. In this direction, Panchayati Raj/ Municipal institutions came into being through the 73rd and 74th Amendments in the constitution passed in the year 1992. This was a radical shift of power from the Centre to Panchayati Raj institutions and urban local bodies both politically and financially. Prior to this, India adopted Liberalization, Privatization and Globalization in 1991 with the presentation of Union Budget in 1991. It was a shift away from license raj to entrepreneurial development, socio-economic, legal, and politico reforms. Thus, our constitution has moved away from unitary to federal reforms to make it more egalitarian. The economic reforms of 1991 pushed India's growth and foreign exchange. As federalism is the soul of democracy, the government had thought of decentralization of power in governance for inclusive growth of deprived sections of society.

But the present regime since 2014 has reversed the process of decentralization. During the last 70 years of democratic rules in India, we never faced such acute problems of federalism as we witnessed from 2014 to

2023. Given below we have come across many instances when there is abuse of federalism by the Centre, and the central government has compromised the autonomy of States.

Ever since the AAP party came into power in Delhi in 2015, the government is at loggerheads with the centre. Since Delhi is not a full-fledged state, Land, Police and Public Order are under the jurisdiction of the LG. Delhi government has been demanding a full-fledged state so that it can even have control over Land, Police and Public Order. It was for the first time that the Supreme Court in its judgement on July 4, 2018, stated that "real power must lie with an elected government" and that the LG was "bound by the advice of cabinet"(BBC, 2018). Delhi is unlike other states that have full control of administrative powers. The court added that the LG could only make independent decisions in matters relating to land, police and public order. It appeared that it was a landmark judgement and that it is a 'win for democracy.' But the elected government was not given the power to rule.

Delhi became the glaring example of a violation of federalism when the Centre enacted a law which curtailed the democratically elected government of Delhi after transferring the decisive power to the Lieutenant Governor (The Economic Times, 2021). When the BJP was rejected by the people of Delhi in 2020, the BJP sought curtailment of the powers of GNCT (Government National Capital Territory). This led to another kind of confrontation between the state government and the Centre.

The rallying point was that the LG has usurped the power of a democratically elected government. The LG started to take decisions on issues other than Land, Police and Public Order. He violated the constitutional norm of "the constitutional head being bound by the advice of the council of ministers." Administrative control of bureaucrats was the main reason for the furore between the LG and the Delhi government. In utter disregard of his constitutional responsibility, he directly held his meetings with the government officials. Naturally, there was chaos as the development works were seized in such a deadlock. In the process, it was the public that suffered due to the lack of development. Quality up-gradation of education also suffered. When the AAP won a majority in the Municipal Corporation of Delhi, it opened another battle with the LG. The LG nominated 10 BJP aldermen who hold significant power and play an important role in the elections of Standing Committees, MCD in-house and ward committee meetings. In a nutshell they have direct control over the MCD.

The federal government led by Modi has been supporting their LG as he is their appointee. Being Delhi as the national capital, the government wants full administrative control and it must have the final say.

But the LG at the behest of Central Government did not like to share power and hence wanted supremacy over the government. Hence, fresh deadlock started especially after the appointment of V K Saxena as LG of National Capital Delhi in May 2022. In another landmark judgement of Supreme Court, the CJI on May 11, 2023 gave the verdict that "the Delhi government had both executive and legislative jurisdiction over 'services' that would enable the government to decide bureaucrats' postings and make them accountable to ministers. The court also ruled that the LG being the centre's representative is bound to act on the aid and advice of the 'council of ministers' headed by the CM."

But this judgement was also not a smooth ride for the AAP government as it had to wait for union notification by the central government before they could materialise their transfer orders. Meanwhile, the Central government brought out an ordinance to halt the power transferred to the Delhi government. A new Ordinance named Government of National Capital Territory of Delhi (Amendment) Ordinance 2023 came on May 19, 2023, to claim of power over services in the capital (Khan, Khadiza. 2023). But this ordinance has to be ratified by the parliament in six weeks' time when both houses are in session.

The latest ordinance has created a statutory body consisting of the CM and two senior bureaucrats which will make recommendations to the L-G regarding "transfer posting, vigilance and other incidental matters." Not only the LG can reject the recommendations of the body, but the body would decide on matters by the majority. This means that the two senior bureaucrats could technically overrule the elected chief minister of Delhi. Naturally, this ordinance has boomeranged the table against the judgement of the Supreme Court that empowered the Delhi government to have jurisdiction over the legislative and executive matters over "services."

Thus, it is very obvious that the purpose of this ordinance is to overpower the elected government that was established by the rule of law. It appears that this ordinance is like contempt of court. When the Supreme Court has given clear-cut verdict in favour of the Delhi government regarding legislative and executive powers over "services", the promulgation of an ordinance against the SC judgement is like the establishment of supremacy over the judiciary which is against the spirit of the constitution. Such conflict between the federal government and the Supreme Court will lead to anarchy and it would have long-term implications of the discord of the two parameters of the Constitution. It gives a very bad message to the people that the judgement of the Supreme Court is not acceptable to the government. The duly elected government loses its importance in a democracy.

The ruling party at the Centre dictates terms with the State governments. It is more so when there are opposite parties at the Centre and at States. Even during the Congress regime, there used to be interference by the Centre which was against the holy practice of federalism. But in recent times, since the 2014 formation of BJP rule at the Centre, there are severe violations of the principle of federalism. There have been recurring controversies about Governor's role in State politics. Since the BJP for the first time got a thumping majority in the 2014 parliamentary election, and they do not want to lose power, they want to uproot the grand old party of the Congress. Therefore, the BJP deliberately adopts unconstitutional methods – coercive methods of horse trading, purchasing of members of the legislative council, defection in opposing party, and toppling the government by abuse of power through the Governor.

Now, the Governor's post is not above board. Rather, the Governors are acting as representatives of the ruling party at the Centre. During the last few years, the governors of Karnataka, Madhya Pradesh, Kerala, Maharashtra, and West Bengal have played their roles in such an egregious way as to make them highly controversial without necessarily adding to the glory of the house. The Governors are found in such shameful activities as non-cooperating with the duly elected governments, delaying the money bill which deprives the development at the ground level, working as an agent of the Centre, and above all sending an adverse report of law and order to the Centre for the imposition of President's rule in the States. Such irresponsible role of governors put development in abeyance.

Prior to 2014, undue interference from the Centre was few and far between. But after 2014 when the BJP came an absolute majority, it misused its power in toppling the State governments where there are opposite party rule. The most glaring example is the governor of West Bengal who has crossed all limits of impropriety, and he has proved to be the agent of the Centre.

S. R. Bommai v. Union of India was a landmark judgment of 1994 of the Supreme Court of India of Centre-State relations, where the court discussed the provisions of Article 356 and related issues under which the President's rule is imposed by the Centre (Sonalli, 1994). The judgment put restrictions on the whims of the governor in dissolving the Legislative Assembly of the State. This action has to be ratified by both houses of parliament. An assembly can be dissolved only when the contending CM loses it on the floor of the house. Since then this judgment is most quoted as it puts a rider on the arbitrary imposition of the president's rule in States.

But even after this safeguard, we find that there are many loopholes which are used to discriminate against a duly elected assembly. This is what we find after 2014, and more so after 2019, when the BJP exercised its power to topple the government of opposite parties. There is moral turpitude as the foremost interest of the BJP is to stick to power and take all measures fair or foul to dismantle the opposite government. It is alleged that since the party has held over the judiciary, things move in favour of the BJP only. There have been many instances when the executive has compromised the judiciary.

The most glaring violation of centre-state relations was the demonetization of ₹500 and ₹1000 which was announced by Modi without taking the stakeholders into confidence. It is now 'fait accompli' that even the RBI was not consulted before the demonetization was announced. The autonomy of the Reserve Bank of India was compromised when the statutory reserves of the RBI were taken over by the central government.

There have been cases of governors sitting over bills and creating hurdles in a smooth flow of democracy as delaying a bill is like delaying the development work. The most glaring example is of Tamil Nadu governor Mr. R N Ravi who finally relented in withholding the bill (Janardhanan, Arun. 2023). Unless the centre supports the governor, no governor would misuse his power and act like an autocrat. This phenomenon is very common in the case of states where the elected government is of another party that does not have alliance with the BJP.

Of late, the Supreme Court's collegium's recommendation of judges of the High Court is gathering dust in PMO (Deccan Chronicle, 2023). The SC collegium has once again sent a reminder on 21st March 2023 to the Ministry of Law. The erstwhile Union Law Minister Kiran Rijiju had raised controversy by calling the 'collegium' opaque. He wanted a government nominee in the collegium to make the system transparent in the appointment of judges of the High Court and of the Supreme Court. The incumbent Vice-President Dhankar has made a scathing attack on the Supreme Court by making a statement that 'Parliament is supreme' as it is the Constitution that is supreme (Outlook, 2023). Dhankar even went on to 'criticize the scrapping of the NJAC Act in 2015 at the 83rd All-India Officer's conference in Jaipur and questioned the landmark 1973 Kesavananda Bharati case verdict, saying it set a wrong precedent and that he disagrees with the Supreme Court ruling that Parliament can amend the Constitution but not its basic structure.' One fails to understand how a person like Dhankar who graduated from law and has held very respectable positions in the government of India would pass such comments and create controversies unethical to the constitution. It is assumed that such statements must be in line with the highest executive command from the PMO.

In a federal country, autonomous institutions strengthen democracy, and they are 'sine qua non' for its existence. But after 2014, we find attacks on the autonomy of institutions. Now, there are no institutions which can claim to be autonomous and without the interference of the centre. The universities are no more autonomous. Teachers do not have the freedom to be critical of any government policy which is not good in the long-term perspective of the nation.

******

Erosion of Democratically Established Institutions

Democratically established institutions are the backbone of democracy. No nation can flourish and develop unless it has thriving and autonomous institutions that have the freedom to shape their roles. Only those nations are strong and powerful whose institutions have the freedom to set their goals. The US is the most powerful because its institutions are strong and its citizens enjoy freedom in playing their roles. These institutions are to be sovereign at the base. There should not be any interference by the government except for their competitive development. In Adam Smith's (1776) parlance, it is akin to a "laissez-faire" system where there is least interference by the government in all activities of the people, varying from the right to choose any economic activities. There is immense cooperation among all entities—social, political, and economic—to pursue one's welfare. Many authoritarian or repressive governments call themselves democratic and yet trample down the democratic rights of people. Our constitution, which has an inbuilt egalitarian character, ensures social, political, economic, and religious freedom.

When the present government led by the BJP does not follow the constitution, as its think tank, the RSS, does not accept the constitution, there is bound to be a disoriented ideology of helping some people at the cost of others. This is what is happening with the present BJP regime, which has reversed long-term egalitarian policy to crony capitalism, a system characteristic of providing benefit to some business groups at the cost of a larger section of society. In order to strengthen our democracy, the government must work hard to improve the performance of democratic institutions. It should think of enhancing public deliberations in democratic institutions. It must improve the system of elections in order to dampen the excessive influence of the groups that are very rich. The government should think about dealing with issues that transcend the boundaries of the nation-state. The government should also improve democratic practices to take account of the internal plurality of our society (NOMOS XLII, 2000). But the BJP government, since its inception in 2014, has involved itself in dividing society along caste and religious lines.

There is no democratic institution in India whose autonomy has not been compromised. There has been undue interference and, hence, decay in institutions of governance.

As usual, each government at the centre has been misusing the ED (Enforcement Directorate), CBI (Central Bureau of Investigation), NIA (National Intelligence Agency), and Income Tax officials for furtherance of its own interests. During the Congress regime, the BJP has been protesting against the misuse of such agencies by the government. Even in the election campaign, Mr. Modi had promised not to harass the common people by such agencies. But such promises were not fulfilled by Modi when he took over as PM in 2014. On record, there are more cases of harassment of common people as compared to the erstwhile regime. The PMO is the most authoritative and autocratic office, where the bureaucrats appear to be puppets of Modi. The last and final word is Modi's *in taking decisions in any ministry. Naturally, his ministry is selected on* his whims rather than the caliber and expertise of ministers. For him, even the ministry of highest importance does not have a comparative ranking vis-à-vis other ministries. It does not matter whether the person heading an important and sensitive ministry has innate qualifications. Smriti Irani, who is just a graduate (as per her information for the 2014 Lok Sabha Elections), was given charge of the Ministry of Human Resource Development in 2014. Later, she became controversial, and she was removed from the Ministry. In the erstwhile Congress government, the HRD Ministry was under the control of great personalities, such as Prof. V. K. R. V. Rao, Prof. Nurul Hasan, Dr. Abul Kalam Azad, Prof. K. L. Srimali, and others. The erstwhile government thought of 'education' as an empowering factor for people, and hence due importance was given to such a ministry. It was because of this great vision that India has progressed well in all spheres of development—economic, scientific, and technical. As Modi himself does not have a higher education, it would be difficult for him to understand how human resource investment plays a greater role in the overall development of the country. The Prof. Kasturi Rangan Report on "New Higher Education Policy, 2020" is the most exhaustive and comprehensive blueprint of prospective education in India, but we are not sure of any competent person in Modi's ministry to take up the challenges of education—all primary, secondary, and higher. The autonomy of academic institutions appears to have been compromised. Quality is no longer the thrust of education; what with higher education? Now, knowledge is no longer the power of our universities; rather, bureaucratic courses and curriculums interfere with the teachers in academic pursuits. Due to interference by the government, low-profile people have started grabbing the coveted posts at universities. These new appointees are biased and do not have scientific reasoning. Hence, during the last nine years, the quality has further deteriorated.

The dream of upgrading our universities and academic institutions to be on par with the best in the world would never be fulfilled unless the government was open to quality education and had a forward-looking attitude towards incorporating structural changes in education.

Modi's recent cabinet expansion in July 2021 was also whimsical, as some very competent ministers were asked to resign among the twelve ministers. Just to cite, I will take one example of Dr. Harsh Vardhan, a cabinet minister of Health and Family Welfare, Minister of Science and Technology, and Minister of Earth Sciences, who was replaced by a very incompetent person, Jitendra Prasad, a state minister. Dr. Vardhan had done exemplary work during the Corona period, but he was shunted out.

During Modi's tenure as India's prime minister, one thing is very clear: the government's agenda is determined much less by the work of ministries and much more by what the leader needs done (Vasudevan, Mukunth, August 4, 2021). Modi has nothing to do with science or scientific temperament; he is interested only to 'the extent he would use science to gain power.'

The mainstream media is under his tutelage. It is under the direct control of the government, which offers them monetary support through government advertisements. There are very few media houses that are objective and do critical reporting. The rest are bootlickers and compromise the objectivity of journalism. The media, or press, which is regarded as the fourth wall of democracy, has a very prominent role in strengthening democracy. It also has a role of vigilance in the other three pillars, viz., the legislature, executive, and judiciary. The media does investigative journalism, which enables any reporter or journalist to narrate the inner story of any event. It harps on the truth for the public. Much of the socio-economic and political development of any country is attributed to the kind of press that functions independently of the government. In fact, freedom of information is the foundation of any democracy. But unfortunately, under the Modi regime, for sheer pecuniary interest, the media has lost its credibility in India.

India has one of the lowest rankings of 142 for press freedom in the world out of 180 countries (RSF, 2021). Even our neighbouring country, Sri Lanka, has a better ranking of 127. Pakistan and Bangladesh are in proximity, with India having RSF rankings of 145 and 152, respectively. It is so shameful for India, which is one of the most dangerous countries for journalists. After Modi again became victorious in the 2019 Lok Sabha General Elections, the index of press freedom remained at 142. There has been no improvement. With the way journalists are tortured, shot, and exploited by the BJP government and its think tank, the RSS, the index of world Press Freedom has gone down. Instead of any improvement in freedom of the press, there has been more deterioration in safeguarding freedom of speech and expression. The so-called conservative and parochial 'Hindutva' has intimidated the journalists and branded them as anti-national or anti-India.

In 2017, Gauri Lankesh, a famous Indian journalist, was killed. Again, five journalists were killed in retaliation in 2020 in connection with their work (Bismee, 2021). This was reported by the US-based Committee to Protect Journalists (CPJ). As Modi appears to be allergic to the truth, he has tightened his grip on the press. The journalists in his regime are exposed to every kind of attack, including police violence against reporters. The way the attacks are made in police presence, with police remaining mute spectators, one can infer that the violence is state-sponsored.

It is under Modi's regime that intolerance has developed. A value system that fosters love, friendship, and affection among people is no longer available. There is too much interference in police activities by the government. The people are not safe. The criminals are scot-free. Since the police are in alliance with the government, there is no guarantee that justice will be done to the aggrieved party. Recently, the CJI Supreme Court is reported to have given its observation that the central investigation agencies like the Enforcement Directorate, the CBI, and the NIA keep the cases in suspension (Mathur, 2021). Perhaps they delay the charge sheet and linger over the cases at the behest of the ruling party at the centre. This situation presents a very precarious situation for law and order. This loses the confidence of the police in India. Recently, Mr. Rakesh Asthana took charge of the Police Commissioner of Police of Delhi before his superannuation two days before, when the rule is a minimum residual period of six months before retirement (Rajagopal, Krishnadas, August 25, 2021). Earlier, he was recommended to head the CBI, but the CJI stopped him from being appointed by the centre. All these show high-handed interference by the government in the personnel law of the police department. This has a demoralizing impact on other honest and impartial officers. Instead of checking such maltreatment and favouritism, the Modi government has encouraged such nepotism, which is detrimental to the impartial functioning of the police administration. Now, the Supreme Court has asked the Delhi High Court to decide the legality of Rakesh Asthana. Here, it is very interesting to observe that Mr. Rakesh Asthana hails from Gujarat, the state where Mr. Modi was the CM for two terms.

Since 2014, society has been divided so much on communal lines that in any incident, the press or media look for a communal angle in any crime. This has led to a very bad reputation for India in the international community, as India is no longer secular and does not care for its minorities (Rajagopal, Krishnadas, September 2, 2021). N V Ramana, the CJI of India, is reported to have condemned the media, saying that a section of it is involved in narrating any incident from a communal angle (The Hindu, September 2, 2021). In fact, as the central government has control over a large section of the media, any incident or crime committed shall get coverage in communal colour in order to further divide the people on communal lines. During COVID-19, the spread of Corona cases in Delhi was attributed to Tabliqui Jamat, a Muslim organisation, as being responsible for the spread of the infection. The Jamat had organised a meeting in Nizamuddin, Delhi, in 2020. In a nutshell, the Muslim people were targeted, which was later found to be false by the Supreme Court. But during the period, enough damage was done to the reputation of the Muslim Community.

The Supreme Court has again criticized the Central Government for its failure to fill a large number of vacancies in tribunals or quasi-judicial bodies. The CJI even went on to make the statement that "the government has no respect for this court." Ramana even warned the government that it was testing their patience. Later, the SC gave one week's notice to make appointments (NDTV, September 6, 2021).

There are a large number of vacancies in critical tribunals like the NCLT (National Company Law

Tribunal) and the NCLAT (National Company Law Appellate Tribunal) over the next two years. These tribunals are important for the economy. Further vacancies in the armed forces and consumer tribunals are responsible for delays in the resolution of cases. This is really very unfortunate when there are millions of cases lying unattended and we do not care to fill up the vacancies, which could have given respite to millions of people in the redressing of their cases.

The police administration is also not independent. There is undue interference by the government at the state level and at the central level. The number of custodial deaths has increased from 2014 to 2019. In recent times, the state government of Uttar Pradesh has withdrawn 20,000 cases of political criminals under a law that is in severe violation of the jurisdiction of the judiciary (Kattakayam, Jiby J. 2018). Yogi is also one such beneficiary. These cases were withdrawn on the ground that they were politically motivated. It is ordinary citizens, not politicians, who deserve the benefit of a review of long-pending cases against them. But Yogi has crossed his limit, as one cannot be a judge in one's own case.

In civil administration, India also does not have a fair system in which officers have the independence to do their best in the discharge of their functions. When the long-standing rule of administration undergoes changes at the whims of an apex body like the PMO, things become adverse. There is suffocation in administrative functioning by each and every functionary. This is what we observe in any department. Hence, the bureaucrats are at their worst. They are demoralized and work under tremendous pressure. Many administrative officers have resigned from the IAS on account of the suffocating environment (The Hindu, September 27, 2019). Kannan

Gopinath resigned in protest against curbs on freedom in Kashmir and the right to dissent. There is a larger question of freedom of expression where the people fail to question the government without being tagged as anti-national. Bureaucrats who owe their allegiance to the constitution are committed to protecting its sanctity. They work in the interests of the State and the people. But if the State becomes dictatorial against the welfare of the people, the bureaucrats come in to protect their guarded rights. In this context, there should be more freedom and autonomy in the administrative service. It was not for his personal agenda that Kannan resigned; he resigned for a larger edifice of national interest. Another example is that of S. Serikanth Senthil, an IAS officer from Karnataka, who resigned and stated that the "fundamental building blocks of a diverse democracy are being compromised." Earlier, some officers used to resign from the central services on personal grounds, not on larger issues as they do now. There is growing unhappiness among people against the State these days.

In its most recent move, the PMO led by the Principal Secretary to the PM, Mr. P. K. Mishra, called for an informal meeting with the Chief Election Commissioner, Mr. Sushil Chandra, and the other two members, viz. Rajiv Kumar and Anup Chandra Pandey, on November 16, 2021 (Chopra, Indian Express, December 17, 2021). Although the CEO raised objections to the meeting, later on he joined the meeting. This was a blatant violation of the independence of autonomous institutions in India. The three people, despite their reservations, had an informal meeting on electoral reforms. This is atrocious and akin to summonses that breach precedent and constitutional norms. The three people were reported to have discussed long-pending reforms like multiple cut-off dates to facilitate a common electoral roll. Despite the meeting being informal, it raised constitutional impropriety. The three ECs are to maintain an arm's length from the executive to insulate the functioning of the poll panel from any external pressure. The EC's communication with the government on election matters is usually limited to its administrative ministry only. The former three Chief Election Commissioners (CECs) are reported to have expressed their displeasure, and they have said that the government's letter expecting the incumbent poll panel chief to attend the meeting was 'unacceptable' and the subsequent informal discussion with the Principal Secretary to the PM could erode "the EC's image of independence." Former CEC S.Y. Quraishi called this meeting as atrocious. Logically, one would ask "Would the government call the Chief Justice of India along with all other judges for discussion on judicial reforms"? Even the PM cannot call the CEC for a meeting. Such unwarranted power given to the Principal Secretary to the PM would lead to the erosion of authority over democratically elected autonomous institutions, ringing a bell for the murder of our vibrant democracy.

In June 2020, the government announced a new media policy in Jammu and Kashmir that was meant to curtail the freedom of the press. Some journalists who protested the media policy were reported to have stated, "Don't gag the media; we are an equally important pillar of democracy", and "Down with media policy 2020". The objective of this media policy is to kill the local media and build only the government's narrative.

Another glaring example of the dilution of a democratic institution as important as the Election Commission, which is empowered to conduct fair and impartial elections in India, was under controversy when Arun Goel was appointed as CEC (Chief Election

Commissioner) after his voluntary retirement in November 2022, when he was to retire from his IAS service in December 2022. The haste with which the government appoints him speaks of a high-handed, discriminatory decision by the PMO.

The vacancy in the EC arose on May 15, 2022, but the government took no initiative to fill it. It was only when Arun Goel, a 1985-batch IAS officer, got voluntary retirement from service in a single day after his file was cleared by the Law Ministry. Thereafter, a panel of four names was put up before the prime minister, and Goal's name got the nod from the President within 24 hours (The Economic Times, 2022). It appears as if the government was waiting for Goel to take voluntary retirement. It is with this respect that the Supreme Court has intervened and asked the government to send Goal's file to the Supreme Court to check whether there was any hanky-panky in his appointment by the government (Ananthakrishnan, G. 2022).

Modi had promised transparency in his governance, but such measures speak of highhandedness in the functioning of a very serious functionary of our constitution. Furthermore, since Modi's election as Prime Minister of India, the tenure of the CEC has been a year or so, despite the fact that the CEC's mandated tenure is six years. Naturally, the short-term tenure of the CEC would give the government scope for manipulation and to play with the federal institutions in its favour. That is why we find that the Election Commission has failed on many occasions to conduct a free and fair election of candidates without fear.

Again, there is another instance of Mr. Sanjay Kumar Mishra, whose term of directorship as Enforcement Director has been extended for the third time even when the constitution does not permit such an extension. Naturally, such an extension would expect the government to take undue favour in prosecuting its interests, and hence the independence of ED, an important functionary of Indian federalism, is questionable in the Modi regime.

There is no official database of Bills put up for public consultation in Parliament under the Modi regime. The TMC MP, Derek O'Brien, cites independent research to prove that only 74 of the 301 Bills introduced in the parliament from 2014 to 2021 have been put up for public consultation. Of these 74 Bills, 40 were not circulated for a duration of 30 days, as is the specified policy (The Hindu, December 16, 2022).

To conclude, one can state that the federal democratic institutions are no longer independent and autonomous, and there is a constant threat to their existence by the government.

******

Human Rights Violations

India is a signatory to the UN Universal Declaration of Human Rights 1948. In the preamble, we find fundamental human rights to be universally protected by all nations big or small, rich or poor. Recognition of inherent dignity and of the equal and inalienable rights of mankind is the foundation of freedom, justice, and peace in the world, in post-independence era, India was criticized globally for violation of human rights in Jammu and Kashmir by its armed forces. The US and various other countries put pressure on the Indian government to take cognizance of the causes of human rights violations in the country. In addition to the international pressure, there was pressure from within the nation that there should be a law that would deal with the issues related to human rights violations. In view of the above, the government of India introduced the "Human Rights Commission Bill" in the Lok Sabha on May 14, 1992. Later this bill was referred to the Parliament's Standing Committee on Home Affairs. In order to cope with the international and local pressure, the President promulgated an ordinance named "National Commission on Human Rights" on September 27, 1993. Finally, the bill was passed and the "National Commission on Human Rights Act" came into being on September 28, 1993. India is the most heterogeneous country having diverse social systems, and people of different faiths varying from Hinduism, Islam, Christianity, Jain, and Parsi, to other ethnic faiths, India is bound to have some problems with violations of human rights. If uniform law and order which guarantees civil, political, cultural, economic, and social rights is enforceable properly, our democracy would have the least cases of violations of human rights. Sometimes, the federal and state governments become mute spectators to atrocities resulting in violations of human rights. Article 21 is the life and liberty clause of the Indian Constitution. But this constitutional guarantee has not percolated to the common people. Inter-religious and caste differences are now more accentuated than ever before. Untouchability has not been banished totally from modern and free Indian society. But ever since the National Commission on Human Rights was established, we found the listing of such human rights violations and efforts were made to address the deprived sections of people. Basic human rights must be provided to the disadvantaged and deprived sections of society. If it is not ensured the structure of the political democracy may blow up. Naturally, most of the economic welfare measures of providing reservations in government jobs to deprived sections of people were made by the erstwhile government only. Still much remained to be done. But the imposition of emergency in India on 25th June 1975 by PM Indira Gandhi across the country led to violations of human rights as thousands of protesters of opposition parties were put in jail. Civil liberties were suspended and the press was censured. Several other human rights violations were reported when there was mass vasectomy of youth. Thereafter, there was the regime of the Janata Party which could not continue beyond two years. Janata Party fell because of its own contradiction of inner bickering. Again, Mrs. Gandhi became the PM in 1980 and continued till 31st October 1984 when she was assassinated. Mrs. Gandhi had got a tough lesson and hence during her regime from 1980 to 84 she cared for the justice, liberty and equality of people. Since then her followers of the Congress Party continued to work for the welfare of the people without any discrimination. Again, it was Narasimha Rao Government that established the National Commission on Human Rights in 1993. Hence, the erstwhile government has taken up issues of human rights violations in India.

But now we find that there are serious cases of violation of human rights in India during the Modi regime since 2014. The BJP speaks ill of the 'declaration of emergency' but in real practice, they have an undeclared emergency in which honest and silent protesters of the present government policies have been put in jail without any charge sheet. The number of custodial deaths has increased. There are unlawful and extrajudicial killings perpetrated by the police. There is degrading human treatment by the prison officials contrary to the norms established for prisoners (The US State Department of Human Rights Report on India, 2021). The government has increasingly harassed people who are rights defenders, activists, journalists, academics, students, and other people who are critical of the government and its policies. In Jammu and Kashmir ever since its bifurcation into two union territories Jammu and Kashmir and Ladakh in August 2019, the Muslims have been tortured (Roth, Kenneth World Report, 2021). Hundreds of people remained detained without charge in Jammu and Kashmir under the draconian Public Safety Act, which permits detention without trial for up to two years.

As India is a multiparty federal parliamentary democracy each state and union territories are duty bound to maintain law and order and the central government must give policy guidelines for this. At present, the US government agencies, the UN, and some nongovernmental organisations identify India as the site of numerous human rights abuses (Congressional

Research Service, 2023). Sometimes, the violations are very significant. Some human rights violations are seen as perpetrated by agents of state and federal government. These violations increased after the re-election of the Modi government in 2019. Some political scientists warn of the backsliding of democracy in India. For example, since 2019, the Sweden-based Varieties of Democracies project has classified India as "an electoral autocracy"; in 2023, it called India "one of the worst autocracies in the last 10 years" (Ibid). France-based 'Reporters Without Borders' (RSF) 2023 Press Freedom Index ranks India 161st of 180 countries, down from 150th in 2022. RSF says that there is continuing downward trend. RSF finds charges of defamation, sedition, contempt of court and endangering national security are increasingly used against journalists critical of the government, who are branded as 'anti-national.' According to Freedom House, "attacks on press freedom have escalated dramatically under the Modi government," with Indian authorities using various laws to quiet critical voices in the media. In India, media takeovers by oligarchs close to Prime Minister Modi have jeopardised pluralism (RSF, 2023). The RSF finds that in the case of India, the situation has gone from 'problematic' to 'very bad.' The other countries which are in the "very bad" category are Kajikistan (153rd) and Turkey (165th). Since 2021, US-based non- profit Freedom House has redesignated India as "Partly Free" contending that "Modi and his party are tragically driving India towards authoritarianism."

As per 2011 India Census Report, there are 79.8% Hindus and 14.2% Muslim out of 121 crore population. The decadal growth rate of Hindus fell to 16.8% in 2011 from 19.2% in 2001. The decadal growth of Muslims fell to 24.60% in 2011 from 29.52% in 2001 (Census, 2011). There are other minorities like Sikh, Jain, Buddhist etc.

live in India. But during 2022, the Human rights Practices Report (HRP Report, 2022) states that throughout the year 2022, there were attacks on members of religious communities, including assaults and intimidation. Where there is double engine government, the members of "Cow Vigilant", ABVP (Akhil Bhartiya Vidyarthi Parishad), and VHP (Vishwa Hindu Parishad) get unwarranted power.

In June 2021, the government announced a new media policy in Jammu and Kashmir, which was meant to curtail the freedom of the press. There were restrictions on internet communication. In fact, the lockdown of August 2019 led to the loss of the economy to the tune of US$2.4 billion. The government took no effort to redress the loss. Losses nearly doubled when the government took measures to check the spread of Covid-19 in March 2020. When the Supreme Court raised the issue of the internet in Jammu and Kashmir as the issue of suspension of fundamental rights, the government lifted the control but it was confined to 2G mobile services which hurt the Covid-19 response.

It is very shocking to know that India has topped the list of countries that resorted to government-imposed internet shutdowns (The Hindustan Times, Feb 28, 2023). The government may impose an internet shutdown on account of "public safety" and "public emergency." But in most of cases in the Modi regime, such rights have been violated for discriminatory political reasons that go against the rules laid down or against the Supreme Court Guidelines. There is no government source that would tell how many times and of how much duration the internet clampdown was made. It is left to the government to find out the economic implications of the shutdown of internet facilities. In this digital world, the internet shutdown would severely affect trade and career opportunities. Owing to this, many brilliant students have been deprived of business and career opportunities. In all ruling states of BJP, it is alleged that there cannot be fair and free reporting of violations of human rights in different forms. The recent violence in Tripura where a Masjid was torched on 26th October 2021 speaks of hatred created by the ruling BJP against the Muslim community. The VHP, a strong ally of the BJP had undertaken a huge procession of Hindus and other religious outfits against the Muslim community in protest against the recent attack on the Hindus in neighbouring Bangladesh. The BJP came to power in 2018 only after 25 years rule of by communists in Tripura. The BJP mixed religion with politics to capture power (Srivastava, Nitin, 25 November 2021, BBC). The BJP in all its ruled states tries to divide the societies on religious and communal lines and then exploit the differences to gain leverage in election. The motto of the BJP is just to grab power for their sustenance only. The two Delhi-based lady journalists Samridhi K Sukanya & Swarna Jha who wanted to give impartial reporting of the incident were arrested and later released on bail. The local administration alleged that the two reporters wanted to disturb the social harmony of the area.

In general, there are five types of human rights violations in India. They are caste based discriminations and violence, communal and ethnic violence, violence related to freedom of association and freedom of speech and expression, violence against women, and violence against children's rights. Such human rights violation is a curse to our society, culture, and humanity.

There were 13,275 cases of drug trafficking in 2014 against 10,631 in 2013. This is an increase of 24.9% over 2013. There was a substantial increase in atrocities against ST communities during 2014 against 2013. The atrocities in 2013 were 6,793 which increased to 11,451 in 2014. The substantial increase was 68.6% of atrocities on ST communities. This is just evidence that the BJP government did not care much to check the atrocities against the ST communities.

During 2019, a total of 4,05,861 cases of crimes against women were reported showing an increase of 7.3% over 2018 (3,78,236).

In 2019, there were 125 deaths in police custody in India. Of this, there were 14 deaths, the highest from Uttar Pradesh followed by Tamil Nadu and Punjab with 11 deaths each.

Setup in 1986, the NCRB (National Crime Report Bureau) is a repository of information on crime and criminals which are used by investigators and planners for improving law and order and also take appropriate measures for the prevention of crimes and maintaining peace and social order. We would be surprised to know that crimes in the Modi regime are unabated and is on gradual progression as compared with the Congress Regime. Since the inception of government formation in 2019 at the centre, we find that the crime related to the atrocities of Scheduled Castes and Scheduled Tribes increased in 2020 over 2019. A total of 50,291 cases were registered for committing crimes against Scheduled Castes (SCs) showing an increase of 9.4% over 2019 (45,961 cases). The crime rate registered showed an increase from 22.8% in 2019 to 25.0% in 2020 (Table-7A.1, NCRB Report, 2021).

Regarding Scheduled Tribes, a total of 8,272 cases were registered showing an increase of 9.3% over 2019 (7,570 cases). The crime rate increased from 7.3% in 2019 to 7.9% in 2020. (Table- 7C.1, NCRB Report, 2021)

Owing to a lack of monitoring and surveillance of digital data, Cyber Crimes increased during the preceding year. A total of 50,035 cases were registered under Cyber Crimes showing an increase of 11.8% in registration over 2019 (44,735 cases). The crime rate increased from 3.3% in 2019 to 3.7% in 2020 in this category. During 2020, 60.2% of cyber- crimes cases registered were for the motive of fraud (30,142 out of 50,035 cases) followed by sexual exploitation with 6.6% (3,293 cases) and Extortion with 4.9% (2,440 cases)(Table-9A.3, NCRB Report, 2021).

Since India does not have a rigorous plan of "Climate Change and its Adaptation" we find an increase in offences related to our environment. During 2020, a total of 61,767 cases were registered under environment-related offences as compared to 34,676 cases in 2019 showing an increase of 78.1%. The cases registered under the Cigarette and Other Tobacco Product Act (COPTA) with 80.5% (49,710 cases) were the highest followed by Noise Pollution Act with 11.8% (7,318 cases) (Table 11.2). A total of 4,05,861 cases of crimes against women were reported during 2019 showing an increase of 7.3% over 2018 (3,78,236) as per NCRB Report 2021.

In 2014 the crime rate per lakh population was 229.2 which increased to 241.2 by 2019. This is a rise of 5.23% over 2014.

On fake Indian Currency Notes in 2019 currency notes 2, 87,404 were recovered whose values were ₹25, 39,09,130. As compared to this in 2020 under (FICN), a total of 8, 34,947 notes worth ₹ 92, 17, 80,480 an increase of 190.5% (Table 208.5, NCRB, 2021) were recovered.

There have been large-scale mass students protests in most of the universities against the infringement of right to expression. On 3rd March 2015, in JNU, Kanhaiya Kumar in the midst of students had expressed his views that he wanted freedom from the RSS which was trying to divide the nation. His expression was in fact freedom within India and not from India. His speech was construed as the speech of sedition against India by the university administration. Though he was arrested, later on, he was released on bail as his speech was doctored. India Today reported that in the original video, Kumar was asking for the end of social evils such as caste and communalism, and was not raising any anti-national slogans (India Today, 2016). Mr. Omar Khalid and Bhattacharya were also released who were arrested after Kanhaiya. Political dissent is not a crime and students have the right to protest against the tyrannical law. Ever since the Modi government was established at the centre, the centre with the help of the police administration has tried to suppress the students' movement. The other glaring examples of suppression of students protest have been from FTII (Film and Television Institute of India), Pune, Jadavpur University, West Bengal, Hyderabad University, Jamia Milia Islamia, New Delhi, Banaras Hindu University, 2017, Aligarh Muslim University's Jinnah's portrait controversy, 2018, and most recent protest in Allahabad University over 400% fee hike for undergraduate courses. As established by laws, universities are autonomous institutions where the government cannot interfere in existing laws without proper legislation and discussions. Given autonomy the universities become knowledge creators, which in the long term serve in the quality development not only of education but of an entire nation in terms of production and employment generation.

A welfare-oriented government would like to lower the crime rate for establishing peace by non-discrimination of existing law and order. The principle of maximum social advantage works on minimizing taxation and in return provides welfare in terms of an increase in amenities, increase in employment generation, and investment in public utility services like roads, schools, transport, and communication for more productivity. But during the Modi regime, there is more taxation and welfare returns is much lower. Only a few business enterprises are the beneficiaries of the uneven income distribution policy of the government. His policy of digitization and ease of administration has benefitted crony capitalists only. In the US, there is anti-trust law that checks the monopoly or group interest of profit motive attitude of capitalists (Chen, May 02, 2022). This law encourages fair competition among entrepreneurs for the maximization of welfare. The present regime in India is unlike the US anti-trust law where the government has been giving all industries to a select few capitalists. This is against the economic empowerment and social inclusion that our constitution guarantees. This is also very much like an infringement of the human rights of the people.

The stand of the BJP government on CAA (2019) and NRC is also very controversial. There were mass protests all over India against the CAA as the CAA is mandated to grant fast-track citizenship to non-Muslim undocumented immigrants from Afghanistan, Bangladesh, and Pakistan. The protesters, activists, and other supporters of anti-CAA movement were charged under India's stringent "anti-terror" law. There was bulldozing of houses of people involved in such protests. It was like Israel's bulldozing of shelters for Palestinians. It was meant to introduce a sense of precarity into the lives of Modi's critics. Modi's critics have a precarious life in India. It has become increasingly hazardous to oppose the policy of the BJP (Sen, 2021).

In 2020, Amnesty International was forced to cease its operation in India as a result of a government –watch-hunt against human rights organisations —uncovered a hacking campaign targeting human rights defenders in the country. Although India is a party to the "International Covenant on Civil and Political Rights," discrimination continues.

In 2021, spyware Pegasus developed by the Israeli cyber security company NSO was used to snoop on opposition politicians, journalists, bureaucrats, academics, and activists in India. Such spyware is sold to only sovereign nations. India purchased this spyware to snoop on opposition leaders, journalists, bureaucrats, academicians, and activists for its own benefit.

Recently, one BJP legislator of Bihar, Mr. Hari Bhusan Thakur made a statement that the centre should withdraw the voting rights of the Muslim community and make them second-class citizens. Such an unwarranted statement from a lawmaker is tantamount to proving that the BJP does not have respect for the Indian constitution and by such a provocative statement the BJP meant to incite communal riots (Deccan Herald, Feb 24, 2022).

It is shocking to know that Akar Patel, chief of Amnesty International was charge-sheeted by the CBI under a money laundering case. When he challenged, the Delhi High Court asked the CBI Director to take back the lookout notice of Akar Patel (Satyahindi.com/ India-Delhi-court, 7/4/2022). There is another very shameful incident of 'journalists had to stand naked for reporting against MLA in MP.'

Every day or so, the government is interfering in the day-to-day functioning of elite academic institutions. Now, the appointment of VCs (Vice Chancellors) of universities by the Governor has become arbitrary. The Governor is supposed to take the concurrence of the government in appointing the Vice-Chancellors. But the

Governor does not look into academic merit; rather he appoints on the directive of the high command of the PM office. In the recent controversy of Chennai, the CM snatched the power of the Governor in appointing the VCs (The Hindu, 26/04/2022). In most Indian Universities, it is the Governor who is the appointing authority of the Vice-Chancellors with some exceptions in some states like Gujarat (1949) and Telangana (1991). In Gujarat and Telangana, it is the government which is the controlling authority of all the universities. On this basis, when there was undue interference from the Governor in the smooth running of the universities in Tamil Nadu, the CM took the decision by the state legislation to clip the power of the governor of appointing the Vice-Chancellors (The Hindu, 26/04/2022). Such trends are unhealthy that go against the ideals of federal laws. This would lead to anarchy in the higher education system. Here, Modi does not seem to protect the federal structure, rather he has weakened by being a mute spectator. There has been a constant and rigorous attempt to collapse the autonomy of the higher education system. During the last nine years, there have been indirect efforts to saffronize the higher education institutions that seek to implement a non-secular Hindu nationalist agenda. There is no end to such intermittent interference in due procedures. Earlier, there was the sanctity of looking into the recommendation of state governments in the appointment of Vice-Chancellors. This government has eroded the long-established procedures of maintenance of quality and execution of fair practices.

The most recent blot of human rights violation is Manipur where there are flagrant violations of human rights since May 2023 without any break. Law and Order have completely collapsed. The Centre and the federal government of Manipur could not save the lives and livelihoods of people. There was the parading of two naked women and sexual assault in strife-ridden Manipur to perpetrate violence in communities. Taking *suo motto* cognizance of the incident Chief Justice of India D.Y. Chandrachud stated, "What matters is that this is just simply unacceptable... This is the grossest of constitutional and human rights violations... We are expressing our deep concern..." (RAJAGOPAL, K. 2023). We will give the government a little time to take action or we will take action," the Chief Justice warned.

To conclude, we can state that considering the vast diversities unparalleled in the world, it is very difficult to ensure justice, fraternity, and equality for all people. In spite of the assertion of protection of life and personal liberty in our constitution which is available to every person and foreigners alike, we find that during Modi's regime from 2014 to 2019 and again in the post-2019 period instead of minimising the violations of human rights, the cases have got accentuated especially after 2019. As the trend shows, we are moving towards an authoritarian regime. Our democracy is backsliding. It is very shameful. We must rise above narrow parochialism and identify ourselves as the most secular democracy in the world.

******

Utter Disregard for Farmers' Problems

The other grave problem that our nation is facing is the pitiable conditions of farmers which Modi failed to address. He was so indifferent to the farmers' agitation that he did not speak or utter a single word of sympathy to farmers. The farmers are the backbone of our economy in terms of their contribution to national income and to a large extent in the employment generation of rural youth. But the Modi government practically failed. In the midst of the Covid-19 pandemic when our economy was going downward below 24 percent (MoSPI, 2020), the Modi government passed three draconian agricultural bills viz. 1. Farmers' Produce Trade and Commerce (Promotion and Facilitation) Act, 2020; 2. Farmers' (Empowerment and Protection) Agreement on Price Assurance and Farm Services Act, 2020; and, 3. Essential Commodities (Amendment) Act, 2020. Their ratifications by the President were done in great haste. So far, agriculture was the only sector that has a 3% growth rate whereas other sectors have languished in India. While I was a research scholar in BHU during 1980-83, I wrote one research paper on "Pricing Policy of Agricultural Commodities in India" which was published in "Yojana" in July 1982 (Sharma and Mishra, 1982). The main objectives of the pricing policy of agricultural commodities among others are threefold. First, the farmers must get remunerative prices for their produce. Secondly, the consumers must not suffer i.e. the price should not be beyond the purchasing power of the common man. Finally, the nation must be on a growth path so that a maximum of people in the rural sector get full employment. The other objective was to make India self-sufficient in food production. Since agriculture comes in an unorganised sector, it is very essential to safeguard the interest of farmers by ensuring them minimum support price (MSP) and providing them markets near their villages for their convenience selling. Naturally, a network of thousands of Agriculture Price Market Committees has been functioning. So far, we have seen good results and the agriculture sector has been giving good outputs. It has also absorbed unemployed youths in the rural sector. Since the Food Corporation of India, a government agency, was working for the procurement of agricultural produces; the farmers were assured of their remunerative price. In spite of all the good features, we can very well understand that there was a dominance of some middlemen who used to eat the remuneration of farmers. But, this too could have been mitigated had the government taken some efforts in checking the middlemen. The farmers are the most vulnerable as they are not organised and they suffer when the monsoon fails. The average size of landholding in India is one hectare for 78% of farmers. Such a section produces 41% of total food production. Their landholding is 33% of the total cultivable land. This shows that these small farmers produce more than the medium and large size farmers. Because of the neglect of agriculture by the government or the authorities, there have been over 17000 suicide cases of farmers during 2018, 2019, and 2020 in different states of India. The suicide cases during 2018, 2019 and 2020 were 5763, 5957, and 5579 respectively. This is as per the report of National Crime Records (NCRB, 2021) 2021 only. This report was shared by the Union Minister of State for Home Ajay Kumar Mishra. Suicide cases were again on the rise during the COVID pandemic.

The current three acts lay emphasis on scrapping the APMC (Agricultural Produce Market Committee) and instead establishing eNAM (virtual National Agricultural Market) in which there is integration of 585 markets across 16 states of India. In due course, all states would be incorporated as the eNAM is gradually extended. The government is also going to do away with the MSP and make farmers are free to sell their products anywhere they desire. The acts perhaps are also meant to liberalize agriculture and make farmers free from different regulations like interference from government agencies with regard to selling their products, provision of minimum support price, and intermediaries like the Food Corporation of India. The kind of agricultural portal which acts visualize is based upon free competition among farmers, who are capable of all electronic procedures of entering the virtual market, getting their produce checked up qualitatively, price fixation of their produce, and getting the remuneration into their accounts. This is not as easy as it appears. We have had a very bad experience with e-governance in India. Still, most farmers are not having banking accounts. It is said that there were around 14.5 crore farmers in 2014-15 of which only 9 crore farmers were identifiable. Of this only 1.31 lakh, farmers got registered for becoming traders. At present, the government has no data on how many farmers are there in 2020.

The acts intend to involve capitalists in farming who would have massive investments in cold storage, warehousing, and advanced technology in agriculture for bumper production. The government is also going to invite 100% FDI in agriculture. All these are meant to make agriculture growth-oriented and hence export-oriented. But with these acts, it is also clear that there is going to be unfair competition with small and marginal farmers. Competition is fair only when the participants have access to all the parameters that play their parts in production. Farmers being non-educated shall be at the receiving end of this production. There is no such agency that will take care of these small and marginal farmers. Even the so-called over-ambitious "Jan- Dhan Yojana" was a flop as most of the accounts remained inactive. The provision of Minimum Support Price for farmers' produce is great succour to farmers in times of hardships and distress. This also acts as an incentive to farmers investing in agriculture. In new acts, there is no provision for MSP.

As agriculture contributes around 16% of GDP with about 40% of the workforce in India, this sector cannot be neglected. Since the surplus labour in agriculture has zero marginal productivity there is a need of shifting surplus labour to other productive sectors of the economy. But due to a lack of infrastructural development, there is a very limited prospect of employment generation. Naturally, the surplus labour of agriculture cannot be shifted to other sectors, and the surplus labour is forced to live in agriculture. Naturally, the productivity of agriculture has to be increased through infrastructural development, improved irrigation facilities, and improved private investments for inclusive growth and improving the living conditions of poor and weaker sections of society. This would also give access to economic opportunity. In order to fulfil the above objectives, we must have a minimum of 4% growth in agriculture in order to feed the entire population and yet provide viable opportunities for surplus labour for their sustenance. It was with these objectives that Swaminathan Committee gave its recommendations in 2006. Prof. M. S. Swaminathan, Chairman of the National Commission on Farmers (NCF) formulated in 2004 to address the nationwide calamity of farmers' suicide in India, had recommended a 50% rise in the weighted average cost of production (Swaminathan, 2006). There are many other quality measures that were supposed to be pursued by the government for productivity in agriculture and the welfare of farmers. But the government has failed to adopt measures for faster and inclusive growth of farmers.

Swaminathan Committee was in tune with the approach to the 11th Five Year Plan (2007-12) which laid thrust on "faster and inclusive growth." It wanted to provide relief to the distressed farmers among whom suicide rates have increased over the years. It recommended reforms regarding land reforms, irrigation, credit and insurance, food security, employment, productivity of agriculture, and farmers' competitiveness. Among others, most important recommendation was to give minimum support price (MSP) to farmers of their produce at 150% of the cost which the farmers accrue. But MSP has been an ad hoc measure of the government and it has not been a legal framework which could protect the farmers from inflation or running costs of different factors of production. By and large the farmers have always been losers. The other supportive programmes of 'crop insurance' and subsidy in electricity supply are rigged with corruption which would not give any relief to farmers. The Food Corporation of India (FCI) which continued to procure agricultural produce from farmers is in debt now. It is to the tune of ₹3.81 trillion which the government has not compensated. Before 2014, the debt was just one-third of what it is now. The erstwhile government was at least supporting the FCI, but the present government has left the FCI to languish. Thus, the fear of farmers is genuine when they conclude that in future, the provision of MSP will be withdrawn forever.

Naturally, the three acts formulated are at variance with the Swaminathan Committee which is very unfortunate. Without looking into the recommendations of the Swaminathan Committee, the launching of eNAM will not lead to a rise in the growth of agriculture and empower the farmers for more investment in the future. The government must play a laissez-faire role in agriculture which does not mean that the government should become mute spectators of the exploitation of farmers by the kulaks. The present acts give prominence to foreign investors and large farmers at the cost of marginal and small farmers.

As the economy of India has run from bad to worse in recent times, the government is finding it very difficult to get revenue from GST. In order to meet the gap between the expenditure and revenue the government has resorted to disinvestment plans in which most public sector undertakings are being privatized, and many public sector banks are being merged. Even the most prominent public utility services undertaking, the railways, is being sold to private enterprises. As unlike agriculture, all core sectors have negative growth, the government wanted dynamism by inviting corporates into agriculture, and making agriculture free from any interference by the State governments. This implies there would be entry of rich traders and private investors in agriculture when the government would withdraw its support to farmers like MSP (Minimum Support Price) and other supportive measures.

So far, agriculture has been on the State List where the state government has the authority to make laws. But the Centre has put agriculture on the Current List with the current acts. This is with a view to having dominance of the Centre over the States in making policy changes in agriculture. Thus, the enactment of three acts is in contravention of established federal norms. If the objective of the Centre is to really help the States to adopt the kind of reforms that would modernize agriculture not only for growth but also to improve the economic status of farmers, check inflation, and have the surplus for food security; it should be welcome. But the present government has the sole objective to benefit the select corporate sectors as evidenced by the rise in food prices, dismantlement of FCI and APMC, and subsequently withdrawal of the MSP. We cannot think of a globalized market for agriculture in India when the farmers are disadvantaged and distressed.

The objective of inclusive and sustainable growth in agriculture is still a distant dream as envisaged in 2007. Just a peep into the history of reforms in the case of the Sugar industry in 1998 showed that private investments did not improve the farmers' productivity or income. State-led deregulation of APMC in Bihar in 2006 did not improve farmers' income or infrastructures. Since 65% of the agricultural produce of farmers in Punjab and Haryana is purchased by the FCI and other State agencies at MSP, the farmers get remunerative prices. The farmers of other States do not get the MSP which makes them poor. Once the farmers have come to know the importance of MSP they too are raising their voices and have joined the farmers' movement. Needless to say, the status of farmers in Bihar has been reduced to that of marginal labourers. The Shetkari Movement of Maharashtra, the apex body of farmers, does not believe in MSP and wants the government not to interfere in price regulation as done by APMC. This organisation that met Mr. Narendra Singh Tomar, the Minister of Agriculture to support the three acts does not want any regulatory agencies by the government. They want the market to play its role to decide the price of agricultural commodities. According to them, the MSP is the real culprit that has weakened farmers. Here, Shetkari Sangathan wants the price of commodities on natural demand and supply. But this concept would go against the ideal pricing policy of agriculture commodities when we intend to check the price equal to the purchasing power of consumers and yet have enough for the public distribution system. In fact, an unregulated market would ultimately lead to a fall in prices as more and more participate. Gradually, marginal farmers would be losers. Therefore, the best thing would be a comprehensive MSP that takes into consideration the farmers' cost of production and fix the price at 50% more than the comprehensive cost. This should be institutionalized to give a long-term perspective of remunerative prices to farmers. Hence, the Shetkari Sangathan must come under the recent farmers' movement in order to give justice to the demand of farmers. They must consider the MSP as the Golden Mean of remunerative prices in order to make the farmers engaged in agricultural activities.

Recently, Nitin Gadkari, former BJP President, in an interview with one news channel stated that the MSP of agricultural produce in India is much above the international price. He was of the opinion that the new laws are beneficial to farmers, and farmers are being misguided. But he is unaware that the subsidies given to farmers in other countries are too substantive. In India, farmers do not get any subsidy. Farmers who constitute 87% of the entire population of farmers have an average income of around Rs. 5000 only (NSSO, 2016). Such farmers have less than 2 hectares of land. These farmers being poor, cannot have bargaining power so as to surpass the corporate sectors who are going to have their own warehouses and dictate terms of trade. Once the laws are adopted, the farmers would be reduced to the farmers of Bihar. Taking into account the escalating cost of inputs into agriculture like fertilizers, irrigation, electricity, and other overhead costs, the incentive of ₹2000 to the PM-KISAN thrice a year is not substantive. The new laws would help only the kulaks who are just 13%.

As the State's Rights of interference in APMC have been taken over by these laws, they are against federalism, which is the basic structure of our constitution. Earlier where States used to play an important role in giving incentives of infrastructure facilities to farmers, they cannot do now as the new laws ask for non-interference. Naturally, welfare measures have been sealed. Farmers who toiled themselves to make India self-sufficient in food security and made ceaseless efforts to develop the green revolution in the 1960s are no more important to the government when the corporate sectors entered this sector. With liberalization, privatization, and finally globalization, welfare centric approach has given way to profiteering. The erstwhile governments did maintain a balance to see that the farmers are not exploited and they are given infrastructural facilities, but now the farmers are at the receiving end. Thus, it is not inappropriate to conclude that the government's attitude has shifted from welfare to profiteering.

In the US, there is an anti-trust law that empowers the government to control and regulate the monopoly of corporate houses for the welfare of farmers. There is no promotion of any single firm in any of the economic activities (US Anti-Trust Laws 2022). In the United States, antitrust law is a collection of mostly federal laws that regulate the conduct and organisation of businesses to promote competition and prevent unjustified monopolies. In India, we do not have such a strong law that prohibits the exploitation of farmers at the hand of large investors. The government since its inception in 2014 has encouraged crony capitalism by giving means of production to a select few businessmen thereby encouraging monopolies.

Naturally, the government must introduce fair competition in agriculture, must continue with MSP, and must have a visible presence to help the farmers before implementing the eNAM portal. As the agriculture sector is unorganised and it has 70% of rural households for their livelihoods, it is very important that this sector of our economy gets full attention from the government. Therefore, agriculture must not be privatized until the farmers are prepared for participate. The present agitation of farmers is genuine as they feel their future is shaken by the non-remunerative prices of their produce.

The yearlong agitation of farmers on the borders of Delhi has proved the solidarity of farmers from all over India. The government did not leave any stone unturned to prove that the agitating farmers are Khalistanis and unlawful people working against the interest of the nation. Although they represented a large section of the farmers' community, the government kept on telling that they represented a minuscule of farmers. According to the government, another large section of farmers supported the three laws against which the farmers were agitating.

******

Economic Policy Framework from Welfare to Crony Capitalism

Prior to the BJP regime of 2014, the Indian economy was based on welfare measures. The principle of growth, equity, and social justice was the hallmark of our economic policy framework. All the factors of production i.e. land labour, capital, and technology were tailored to raise savings, investment, and consumption levels for goods and services in a way congenial to check the gap between the rich and poor. At the time of independence, our savings ratio was too low, our food production was not sufficient to feed the entire population. We had to look towards the US for wheat for feeding our people. Under such adverse circumstances, our first Prime Minister Pt. J. L. Nehru laid the foundation of the socialistic set-up of the economy meant to check the skewed income distribution. As agriculture constituted more than 50% of national income, our first plan of 1951 laid emphasis on agricultural investment. Gradually with good governance and incentives in agriculture, food production rose. Onwards in the second and third five-year plans with the public sector investments in industry and technological development, we became self-sufficient in food production. The savings ratio increased. The Per Capita food production and Per Capita Income increased. Our GDP growth rate came to 3.5% per annum which was most respectable among all the developing countries of the world. This so-called Hindu Growth Rate (K N Raj, late 1970s) of 3.5% remained stable in spite of the fact that the population was growing more than 2%. This growth rate of the population of more than 2% had a depressive impact on our economy as most of our GDP was used in feeding the population and providing a basic service of health, education, and law and order to the people. What was left out was used for development works. Our Public Sector Units like the Railways, Heavy Industries, Transport, and Communication are utility services. Therefore, their prices were regulated and they were kept below the purchasing power of the common man. The taxation policy worked on giving the least burden to the taxpayer and more advantage to him in return by different schemes of government. The Planning Commission, established in 1950, was a non-constitutional body kept the pace of development by way of five-year plans. The PM himself used to be the Chairman of the Planning Commission and monitored the development through a team of experts. In spite of all its success and self-sufficiency in food production, we faced two severe wars with China and Pakistan where our resources were depleted. Because of the deep impact of wars our fourth five-year plan suffered and there were planned holidays during 1966-69. Although, Pakistan was no match to us China taught us a lesson to be very vigilant with China and we must invest in more sophisticated weapons. Naturally, after Nehru, Mrs. Gandhi went for a nuclear detonation test in 1974 in Pokharan which brought India among the comity of nuclear nations.

After liberalization, privatisation, and globalization in 1991 led by the Finance Minister, Dr. Manmohan Singh under the Prime Minister of Mr. P. V. Narsimha Rao, the growth rate picked up. But the privatization was limited to the opening of industries to entrepreneurs for more productivity. The license raj ended and there were reforms in economic, legal and administrative governance to encourage the private entrepreneurs. This led to a rise in exports and decreasing the current account deficit. Our foreign exchange reserves increased which boosted our economy for growth and development. Since 1991, the budget size increased by 19 times and our economy grew by 9 times in 2019. In 1991, our GDP was mere $266 billion and by 2019, this has come to $2.3 trillion (Mudgil, Amit 2018). The basis of growth shifted from plan to market for economic efficiency. But the Public Sector Units constituted an important part of development. A concept of a combination of private and public partnerships emerged to meet the finance for larger investments. The nationalisations of banks of 1969 and 1971 were thought to be bad for the economy. But the government instead of privatisation brought out reforms in banking operations. The core banking and internet-based banking started which led to better unification of monetary and fiscal policy in economic activities. The employment status of rural and urban was in the balance as agriculture was one of the main thrusts of the then-existing regime. Ever since the BJP took over its reign in 2014, we find that there is a paradigm shift from 'welfare to profiteering' in all its programs. Although in 1991 with privatization, liberalization, and globalization, there was a shift from plan to market, there was a balance between the two. Public Utility services viz. the Railways, Roads and Transport, etc. were in the government's hands. But, thereafter, to promote crony capitalism, the government is constantly selling public sector units in the name of disinvestments. As public sector units are the lifelines of our economic systems, their prices are regulated to be reasonable within the reach of the common man. But this government in the name of modernization has escalated the price of essential commodities which are beyond the purchasing power of the common man.

In India now, 'crony capitalism' is on the rise (Bouissou, Julien. September 15, 2022). This is evident from the fact that instead of promoting free enterprises, Modi is promoting crony capitalism in India where one per cent of the population owns 33% of the national income. Here crony capitalism means the promotion of a few business houses by the government when most of the other enterprises are not given due attention. Julien refers to Gautam Adani whose assets have grown from $70 million in 2002 to $7 billion in 2014. It may appear to be very good news for India, but the point is there is malfunctioning in the Indian economy where the income distribution has become more skewed, and there is constant promotion of crony capitalism by Modi. Modi has provided an excess of government resources to Adani. Adani has not invented anything remarkable and innovative business model that he should get undue favour from the government. But he is close to the PM that he has been given the conglomerates of airports, ports, mining, aerospace, defence industry, green energy etc. This is true to say that "one man's triumph in politics is another man's success in business". Both Modi and Adani come from Gujarat.

We have discussed in other chapters how the economy has suffered from bad to worse from 2014 to 2019 and thereafter from 2019 to till date because of a shift in policy measures from the welfare of a large section of people to a small section of what we call as 'crony capitalists'. The income distribution is more skewed in favour of the rich than the poor. The Covid-19 pandemic has already ruined the purchasing power of the common people. We have not overcome the deficit in investment for employment generation of 2020-2022. As the public sector units are given to a select few industrialists without regard to the safety of the poor section of people, the price of commodities and utility services would rise beyond the purchasing power of the poor. Hence, the consumption level would fall threatening the production level of manufacturing industries. According to CMIE (Centre for Monitoring Indian Economy), the unemployment rate in India has grown to 7.5% in 2022. Therefore, the most important thing which the government should do is to have a balance of rural and urban sectors in employment generation. Most of the government's flagship programmes of welfare also suffer due to neglect and corruption of administrative machinery.

******

Abetment to Communal Riots

As the principal stand of the BJP is to incite communal riots, especially between Hindus and Muslims, the party has a penchant for dividing the communities on religious lines. Modi, the Prime Minister of India, must break his silence on such issues which are a threat to national unity, but he does not. We can cite many such instances where Modi has failed in his responsibilities as the Prime Minister. One most recent incident is "All Dharma Sansad" at Haridwar in December 2021. There were hate speeches by the so-called Hindu Saints against the Muslim Communities. The hate speeches were even likened to a call for genocide against the Muslims. The Dharma Sansad had the full support of the police administration. Even the speakers who raised inflammatory speeches against Muslims were found to have taken selfies with the BJP leaders. We cannot say that the Dharma Sansad was organised without the permission of the ruling party in Uttar Pradesh. The most prominent speakers who spouted venom against the minority community were Swami Prabodhananda Giri, President of Hindu Raksha Sena called for taking inspiration from Myanmar where the Hindus were being chased away, and the police and government were mute spectators. Just like that the Muslims should be chased away. He went one step ahead and called for the genocide of the Muslim Community. He said, "Since India is now our state now, we must exterminate them". The statements calling for ethnic cleansing and genocide are very alarming given Prabodhanad's connection with the

BJP. The second most prominent speaker was Sadhvi Puja Shakun Pandey who happens to be the general secretary of the Hindu Mahasabha, also called for arms and incitement to genocide (The Wire, 2022). She is also reported to have distributed knives to minor girls on Savarkar Jayanti in May 2019. She also burned the effigy of Mahatma Gandhi in January 2019 and raised slogans in support of Godse, the man who killed Gandhi. Another prominent person was Swami Anandswaroop who is famous for his hate speeches. He is reported to have said that this Dharma Sansad's decision would be the word of God and the government would have to listen to it. If the government does not listen to the word of Dharma Sansad, they would wage war more gruesome than the revolt of 1857. All these are testimonies to the conspiracy against our constitution where, there is a place for each and every individual to live in harmony. No one should be allowed to incite communal hatred against any community or sect or religion. Such people who disturb the peace and tranquility of the nation by involving themselves in dividing people through hate speeches should be prosecuted immediately. But on such occasions, we have not heard of any directive from the PM to shun violence in any of his public addresses. This is very bad on the part of Modi who appears to be fully involved in such nefarious activities to gain political mileage.

The venoms of Dharm Sansad went unabated in organising more such conferences. It is only when the Supreme Court intervened that the second Dharm Sansad at Roorki proposed on 27th April 2022 of Uttaranchal was cancelled.

There is "Genocide Watch", an international institution established in 1999 by Gregory Stanton to watch genocide and take measures to punish the people who abet genocide. It exists to build an international movement to prevent and stop genocide and other forms of mass murder. It has issued an alert on India with regard to Kashmir and Assam (Genocide Watch, 1999). Attempts at genocide would lead to civil war. Some leaders of BJP are glorifying Godse and Savarkar which would again come in hate speeches. Those who glorify Godse and Savarkar must be condemned by Mr. Modi which so far he has not done. (YouTube, 28 Nov, 2019).

The most recent incident is of communal riots of Jahangirpur of New Delhi that took place on the Hanuman Jayanti procession. The incident happened near a mosque where religious slogans were raised in the procession, thereby provoking the Muslim community. There was an attempt to hoist a saffron flag in front of the mosque that infuriated the Muslim Community. There was brick-batting from both sides, but the police arrested only Muslim persons. This shows a clear-cut discrimination of one community against the other community which would ultimately endanger the lasting peace. As many as 12 states (viz. Uttar Pradesh, Gujarat, Madhya Pradesh, Jharkhand, Bihar, Tripura, Manipur, West Bengal, Andhra Pradesh, Maharashtra, Uttaranchal, and Goa also witnessed such hatred translated into arson, loot and vandalism. Even, the JNU was in turmoil over a trifling issue of non-veg food in Kavery hostel on Hanuman Jayanti. It appears there is a constant effort by the rightwing forces supported by the ruling Central government to divide the peace and exploit the emotive cultural or religious issues for the vote bank. Such vandalisms are also meant perhaps to divert the attention of people from rising unemployment, price rise, and cuts in welfare measures. The central government on 30th March 2022 informed the Parliament that India witnessed 3,399 cases of communal or religious rioting during 2016-2020 (Hindustan Times, 2022).

If the established norm of 'law and order' is maintained, there could be no problems of communal clashes and 'peace and tranquillity' would be the order of the day. It appears that there is tacit understanding between the BJP and its right-wing organisations like the RSS and the Hindu Mahasabha to go ahead with the divisive politics and divert the attention of people from economic issues so that the 'vote bank' could be kept intact.

If the BJP government at the center could do nothing on the economic front, it has done much harm in eroding constitutional values and disintegrating social harmony. Its impact has been so catastrophic that another decade or two would be taken to iron out the differences. It is as if we are retreating to the barbaric rule of communal clashes, caste wars, and ethnic discrimination away from development.

Another key feature of this BJP rule government is raising issues of the take-over of mosques by the Hindu Rightwing organisation and changing of names of districts, places and roads in favour of Hindu names. The far-reaching impact of communal hatred of the demolition of Babri Mosque of Ayodhya in 1992 is still not over when we are listening to the call of Varanasi (Gyan Bapi Mosque), Mathura (Shahi Eidgah Mosque) and Agra (Taj Mahal) for takeover by the Hindus. The name of the "Faizabad" district has already been changed to "Ayodhya". The railway station "Mughal Sarai Junction" has already been changed to "Pt. Deen Dayal Upadhyay Junction. Now, Akbar Road, Humayun Road, Tughlag Road, Shahjahan Road etc. are in the process of being renamed in favour of Maharana Pratap, Maharshi Valmiki, Guru Govind Singh, and General Bipin Rawat respectively.

What would our nation get out of such narrow and parochial measures of this government? Such things would inflate communal hatred against one community by the other. Although our nation would get nothing from such measures, our nation would be pushed back to conservative feelings of discrimination, and exploitation on the basis of religion, ethnicity and race differences. Instead of fighting social evils, we would impose such discriminating ideas. The greatest harm would be our policy of universal brotherhood.

Some of the civilized states like Sweden are already watching the day-to-day activities of our nation. To them, India is being converted into "electoral autocracy" from "largest democracy". This is the report by the Swedish V-Democracy Institute. It is now being compared with Pakistan in autocracy. It is as autocratic as Pakistan when it comes to censorship & worse than Bangladesh and Nepal. In 2019 India was counted among the 10 autocratic countries. Since 2019, nothing has improved; India must have gone further down in moving towards a more autocratic state. The right to freedom of speech and expression is at stake. The State does not accept any criticism from the press or any journalist. Now, many are in jail who had peacefully protested against the deteriorating law and order situation in the country (V-Dem Institute, 2021).

Leaders must condemn hate speeches as done by Joe Biden and Kamla Harris on the occasion of the shooting incident in Atlanta in which there were eight murders – six of them Asian women on 17th March 2021. In their solemn speeches at Emory University, Atlanta they reclaimed one of the central roles of recent American Presidents 'which is not only to convey empathy after a tragic incident like shootings, but also to provide moral clarity on matters of race and ethnic diversity'. They decried acts of violence against Asian Americans after a year during which the Trump administration had inflamed racist attitudes. Both tried to illuminate the intimidation, harassment and fear that Asian Americans have experienced during Trump's pandemic year (Reston, CNN, 2021).

Modi never speaks on such occasions. Such violence goes unabated in India without any condemnation by him publicly. He should speak against the inflammatory speeches of hate as done by the right-wing followers of the BJP at Dharm Sansad. He should lay emphasis on cultural harmony which our nation has earned since time immemorial. Our philosophy of "Universal brotherhood" should be reiterated and efforts should be taken by the national government to foster love, affection and brotherhood in times of crisis. Unfortunately, Modi wants to rule; not serve the people. Unlike Biden, he appears to be an immoral leader.

There were hate speeches even by the BJP leaders at the anti-CAA protest in Delhi in January 2020. For BJP cow is more important than men. In many cases, the protection of cows has become a hoax, but it did create hatred among the Hindus against the Muslims and Christians. The Supreme Court is the real saviour and protector of victims of hatred arising out of hate speeches. The Supreme Court bench consisting of two Justices KM Joseph and B V Nagarathna ordered the police of all states to take 'suo motto' actions against hate speeches and further ordered that any hesitation to act in accordance with this direction will be viewed as contempt of court and appropriate action shall be taken against the erring officers (Indian Express, 2023). Hate speech is a serious offence that affects the social fabric of a nation.

If each and every case of hate speech is filed irrespective of religion things would improve and there shall be peace and tranquillity in day-to-day life. If this is strictly followed, there would be no violence in any of the rallies whether it belongs to one religion or other.

India has lost numerous people's lives in fanaticism, hate speeches, and inciting the crowd to violence. Even social ill will created among different castes, religions, sex, region or tribes based on ethnicity leads to violence. Even lawmakers do such things to get leverage against their opponents to get votes for the rule. The present government does not appear to be sacrosanct in its attitude when riots erupt. If the federal government is not purely secular, it will have long-term and far-reaching implications on the lives and livelihoods of people as has happened in Manipur. All should abide by the constitutional provision of solution to any problem.

******

Lack of Welfare Measures, Unemployment, and Poverty

The BJP government was founded on false promises of the creation of 20 million jobs every year. Modi also promised to end poverty by removing black money and sharing some percentage of black money among people, end of rampant corruption, streamlining procedures for investments both private and foreign in the economy, and among others promoting of infrastructural facilities for the farmers. The BJP laid emphasis on inclusive development by the most popular slogan "One India, Best India – Unity and Development of all" (BJP Manifesto, 2014). It was not different from the UPA-II manifesto of 2014 which laid emphasis on the "Empowerment of each hand for progress" (INC, 2014). But what we found from the BJP was utter disregard of the promises and giving importance to some selected industrial houses. This has led to further the economic inequity of resources existing between the rich and poor. Even after nine years of so-called e-governance and ease of administration, there is rampant corruption and there is no creation of jobs. Modi's misadventure of demonetization of ₹500 and ₹1000 in 2016, and unplanned implementation of GST in 2017 ruined the thriving economic structure of savings, investment, demand, and supply. Petrol and oil were not included in the GST as there was a deliberate attempt by the government to deprive the common people of the benefits of declining international oil prices. It was stated that the revenue generated by the declining international oil prices would be used for development. The price of petrol and diesel is much higher than what the UPA government gave to people during 2009-2014. Millions of youths in the unorganised and manufacturing sector were thrown out of jobs due to demonetization. One estimate of the National Sample Survey Office's Periodic Labour Force Survey states that around 5 million people lost their jobs during 2016-18; the job crisis began to worsen. Unemployment was at 45 year high of 6.1% in 2017- 18 which was the reflection of the adverse impact of demonetization (MOSPI, 2019).

Compared to this, during UPA Government from 2009 to 2014, the GDP was in the range of 5.4% to 5.9% in spite of the global recession of 2008. Yet, the agriculture sector during 2013-14 grew more than 4.7%. Balance of payments had improved drastically as the current account deficit came down from US $88.2 billion in 2012-13 to US $32.4 billion in 2013-14. There was record high food production of 264.4 million metric tons and oil seeds of 32.4 metric tons. India had the second fastest growing services the CAGR at 9% just below China's 10.9% during 2011-12 (The Hindu, 2014).

Such a feat has not been achieved by the Modi government. The so-called digitization without proper planning to integrate the common people in the opening of accounts has come as a stumbling block in inclusive development. The government introduced electoral bonds and amended the "Foreign Contribution Regulation Act" which pumped black money into its party's coffer (Department of Economic Affairs, 2015). The election commission virtually failed in controlling the flow of money in the election campaign except by somehow administering the conduct of election procedures. Media houses were funded enough to make Modi's face prominent in all its programmes. Loans of defaulter corporate houses were written off ₹2.4 lakh crore in three years, and in return, the corporate houses donated to the party fund. BJP received over ₹750 crore from corporate, and individual donations; the highest for 7 years in a row (Business Today, 2021). The NPAs of 27 Public Sector Banks increased from 12% to 140% during the last two years (2016-18). As per RBI provisional data on global operations, as of 31.3.2019, the aggregate amount of gross NPAs of PSBs and Scheduled Commercial Banks (SCBs) were ₹ 8,06,412 crore and ₹ 9,49,279 crore respectively. Thus, the total NPA is ₹17.55 lakh crore (US$218.4 billion) as on 31st March 2019 (Ministry of Finance, 24 June 2019). As per the recent estimate, in the second quarter of 2019-20, our economy advanced by 5%. This has slowed down from the earlier position of 5.8%. This slow-down was attributed to the slowing down of the manufacturing and construction sectors.

India has the potential to grow at a much faster rate, but mismanagement by the present government and hastily implemented GST has resulted in this slowdown. Lesser known Infrastructure Leasing & Financial Services Limited (IL&FS) founded in 1987 operated through more than 250 subsidiaries collapsed in September 2018, and it had defaulted ₹90,000 crores (US$12.64 billion) (Anand, 2018). Although the mismanagement and maladministration had already put India out of gear in employment generation and the creation of a favourable environment for saving, investment and income generation, the Covid-19 pandemic gave another severe blow to our economy. Covid-19 from January 20 to December 21 (two years) gave an adverse impact on the parameters of growth and income distribution.

During the first year of Covid-19, since it entered India in January 2020, the government took cares in preventive check-ups and treatment of patients. Therefore, the first phase was not unsatisfactory as she worked in sync with the WHO. The Covid-19 pandemic was very much in control till the first phase which continued till March 2021. But after April 21, India slowed down the Covid-19 campaign due to low cases of Covid-19. A sense of complacency developed. But thereafter in the second phase, Covid-19 cases were beyond control. It was self-inflicted national catastrophe (The Lancet, 2021). "Modi's government seemed to be more intent on removing criticism than trying to control the pandemic" and "Modi's action in attempting to stifle criticism—are inexcusable"(Lancet, 2021). Even Amartya Sen, Nobel Prize Winner of Economics is reported to have stated that the ravages of the Covid-19 pandemic in the second phase were due to Centre's schizophrenia (Sen, 2021).

During Jan 1, 2020 and Dec 31, 2021, we witnessed the highest number of Covid-19 deaths (4.7 million) by the WHO which is the highest in the world (Business Standard, 6th May 2022). The government's figure was 481,486. The WHO figure is almost ten times the official figure of India. Although, the government rejected the WHO report, but there were many lapses on the part of our health ministry in recording the death cases of Covid-19. This has signalled as the collapse of our medical system. It has exposed our five trillion-dollar economy. There is an acute shortage of medical oxygen in most of the hospitals of India. This crisis has endangered the lives of thousands of Corona and other patients who urgently require oxygen for their life support in the ICU and on a Ventilator. Although India is one of the large producers of medical oxygen in the world, the problem is now of transportation.

Who is to blame or share the responsibility for the failure of the logistics of proper planning of the production of medical oxygen and its distribution throughout the length and breadth of India? The moment any crisis emerges, the incumbent government blames the erstwhile government for the failure rather than taking quick action to redress the crisis. A sincere government cannot give such lame excuses. The present government has had seven years of its rule at the centre. Ever since the Corona-19 pandemic gave an impact on India, scientists have been warning of different variants of Corona which are at times more infectious and deadlier. But the government was too complacent to plan health preparedness on February 21 when the new variant started its impact slowly in India. Unmindful of its deeper impact, the government was busy planning elections in five states. A year before, we had seen the plight of migrant labourers during the lockdown period. But this incident was not in perspective by the present government. Again, thousands of migrant labourers started moving to their native places. This time the plight of migrant labourers was more catastrophic as this corona variant was also catching the young population. The Covid-19 pandemic further aggravated our economic crisis when there appeared to be some sign of improvement in the last quarter of 2020. Can India cope with the twin problems of economic crisis and the latest Corona pandemic? Is India now resilient enough to maintain its past growth of GDP, solve problems of acute unemployment, and yet involve in welfare programs starting from poverty removal to the provision of infrastructural facilities to hospitals for treatment of corona and other diseases? The problem of agitating farmers that constitute a very large population for over six months had not yet been addressed by the present government.

The thrust of this party appears to be the escalation of religious sentiments rather than the welfare of people. As the government's machinery could not come out in sync with the gravity of the Covid-19 pandemic, India suffered the most in terms of the highest record of deaths of our people, fall in jobs, and aggravation of medical facilities. Although the PM's Care Fund was exclusively constituted to check the spread of Covid-19, treat its patients and generate infra-structural facilities all over India to come up on par with the best facilities to fight against the pandemic, but its performance was far from satisfactory. Unfortunately, the PM's Care Fund was un-auditable giving scope for manipulation and corruption in the purchase of medical facilities to equip the existing hospitals and care centres. There was a pathetic and indifferent attitude of the present government in redressing of problems of Covid-19 migrant labourers. The situation was so grave that the migrant labourers had to flee from the cities to their homes on foot. The railways and other transport services were completely paralysed. There was no government machinery which could coordinate with the state governments in transporting these migrant labourers. The PM's care fund was nowhere here to provide food and shelter to these labourers.

The demonetization of currencies in November 2016 led to a sudden fall in employment and a lowering of income of people in general and wage earners in particular. This led to a slump in demand thereby leading to a fall of consumption and a fall of investment which in turn led to more unemployment. This has accentuated poverty among wage earners and marginal farmers. The automobile industry has been hard hit. It has thrown millions of people out of jobs. The reason behind this recession is a liquidity crunch, increased prices of products due to regulatory measures, higher taxes and a rise in insurance rates. According to the Society of Indian Automobile Manufacturers (SIAM), during the last three months of 2018 there has been cut of 0.2 million jobs due to a slump in demand of automobile dealerships (Sharma, 2019). The railways will retrench 0.3 million out of 1.3 million employees. Now all airports have been given to select business houses in contravention of the Monopolistic and Restrictive Trade Practices Commission (MRTPC) which was established in 2008 for promoting fair competition among stakeholders. There is again a slump in Fast Moving Consumer Goods (FMCG) such as nondurable household goods like packaged foods, beverages, toiletries and other consumables in rural areas. Hindustan Lever has also shown a deficit in demand (Shyam, 2019). The corporate sector during the last three quarters has shown unprecedented weakening of investment, not because of its borrowing capacity but because of a fall in productivity owing largely to a slump in demand. Even after the reduction of interest rates by the central bank, the investment demand is not picking up. We do not find data on unemployment during 2014-19. There is only available data of the NSS 68th round of 2011-12 (NSSO, 2014).

There are flagship programmes of the Union Government which are approved by the Union cabinet or Development Evaluation Advisory Committee of the Planning Commission (DEAC). They are of utmost importance as they take care of health, education, environment, irrigation, rural and urban development, employment, and other sectors. Some other flagship schemes of this government are (i) Swachh Bharat

Abhiyan launched on October 2, 2014, (ii) Digital India Programme launched on July 1, 2015, (iii) PM Surakshha Bima Yojana launched in 2015, (iv) PM Jan Dhan Yojana launched in August 2014, (v) Beti Bachao Beti Padhao, (vi) PM Kausal Vikas Yojana (PMKVY), and (vii) PM Ujwala Yojana launched on May 1, 2016. These new programmes did influence the rural people, marginal farmers and wage earners which the BJP used as vote banks in the last 2019 general election. All flagship programmes of this government did not fare well. Modi's promise of end of 'open defecation' is nowhere seen. Ujwala Yojana failed because the price of LPG cylinders is beyond the reach of the poor people. This has forced the people to depend on coal which goes against the net zero CO_2. The price of a gas cylinder is now more than ₹1000 which was around ₹450 before 2014 in the UPA regime. The price rise of oil has a cascading effect on food and other essential products which have hit hard the common man. The Indian currency is all-time low against the dollar and pound. The Digital India programme is limited to urban areas only. As crime against women has increased the "Beti Bachao and Beti Padhao Yojana" is a great failure. The PM Kausal Vikas Yojana is not properly coordinated with the manufacturing sector. Although Jan Dhan Yojana of BJP brought 462.5 million people in the formal banking system by 2022 during eight years of its launch in August 2014; it was found that almost 81.38 million of accounts remained inoperative (Moneylife Digital Team, 2022). The basic idea of the launch of PM Jan Dhan Yojana was to make the rural people inclusive in the digitisation process of economic development. But this was very sorry state of affairs of JDY. There is a difference in the overall figure of 78% literacy and its actuality. There is much to be done in rural areas as regards its implementation.

The BJP government scrapped the five-year plans and done away with the Planning Commission in 2015. The Planning Commission has been replaced by NITI (National Institution for Transforming India) Ayog. Earlier, there was five-year plan based on the foresighted view of famous statistician Prof. Mahalanobis. This five-year plan was good as it transformed India from a poor country to one of the fastest developing economies. This period was also very reasonable to check and revise any flaws in the planning. Now, there would be fifteen-year vision of development in tune with global trends and economic growth... The first Vision Document 2031-32, has come out which is in sync with the UN's 2030 Sustainable Development Goals (Panagariya, 2017). This new vision has a mandate to transform India into "a prosperous, highly educated, healthy, secure, corruption free, energy abundant, environmentally clean and globally influential nation" by 2031-32. However, nothing significant has been released in the previous six years since the establishment of NITI Ayog. We will not be able to meet the aim until the factors of growth and development are effectively handled and coordinated. The income distribution is currently more skewed towards the wealthy. We do not have universities which could be regarded as the best in the world. Modi promised to establish ten universities in the public sector and ten universities, in the private sector in 2017 on par with the best universities of the world (Hindustan Times, 2017). Most of Central Universities are starved of staff and resources to upgrade the quality in higher education. What to speak of State Universities? The promise of Modi is like a mirage that cannot be achieved. We have a young population of 65 per cent below the age of 35 years. India does have a vast potential of growth and development. But such demographic advantage cannot be put into dividends unless we improve our infrastructural development and quality improvement in teaching and learning. The most ambitious New Education Policy 2020 has not still been properly formulated to bring in quality changes in our education system. Our health system could not stand the test of Covid-19 which led to maximum deaths in India. The corruption is still very rampant; rather, it has surpassed the existing record in all sectors. Our dependency has increased more on imported oil as its price has shot up due to a shortage of oil. Russian war with Ukrainian also led to a strain on our economic resources. But when the economy was buoyant from 2014 to 2019 due to a fall in oil prices, the government gave no return to people in lowering the oil prices in India.

There has been exorbitant election expenditure by political parties. In the 2019 general election, the expenditure was twice the expenditure done in 2014. The BJP alone spent ₹27000 crore (US$3.8 billion). Such practice would put a genuine and common man away from seeking an election as an independent candidate. There are attacks on long-established federal institutions as there is interference by the governments. The Act of Right to Information has been diluted.

As per the recent IMF study, India had negative real GDP growth of 7.3% during 2020-21 due to Covid-19 pandemic. The economy is reported to have bounced back to the pre-pandemic year of 2018-19. The projected real GDP growth of India during 2021-22 is 9.5% and during 2022-23 is 8.5% (IMF, 2021). Our NSO (National Statistical Organisation May 31, 2022) in its report estimated the growth rate of GDP during 2021-22 to be equal to 8.7% which is less than the projected growth rate of IMF. Naturally, the future growth rate of GDP in 2022-23 will be much less than 8.5% as projected by the IMF. The global recession due to the tightening of monetary policy as a consequence of Russian-Ukrainian war would further lower the growth rate. As per the IMF study, the gross public debt in India during 2020 was 89.6% of GDP. This projected public debt will hover around 90% during 2021-23. As per the IMF, the unemployment rate is 7.1% which is very high (IMF, 2021). The inflation rate was 6.2% during 2020-21 which is much more than the saving and fixed deposit interest rate in banks. When we consider all with the depleting foreign exchanges in recent times, we are left with the sole conclusion that the economy is heading towards a severe debt trap.

As per UN Millennium Development Goals (MDG) programmes, 80 million people out of 1.2 billion which constituted 67% of India's population were below the poverty line of $1.25 in 2018-19.

According to one estimate of the Labour Force Survey, there are 200 million people below the poverty line. There are 230 million people whose Per Capita Income is below ₹375. Again, the unemployment rate at the moment is 7.6% of our population (Hosabale, Duttatreya, October 1, 2022).

There are now limited public expenditures that do not encourage employment generation. Due to digitisation and thrust by the present government to link financial transactions with the Aadhar, we find that millions of rural workers have been thrown out of jobs. The reason is if there is any difference in a letter in the name, the transaction fails. As a result, the wager is left out with no option but to correct the Aadhar Card and its linkage with the Bank account to get the remuneration. The administrative machinery is not skilled enough to rectify the errors. This results in massive corruption in such government-sponsored programmes. MNREGA (Mahatma Gandhi National Rural Employment

Guarantee Act) which came into being in 2005 gives a guarantee of 100 days jobs in rural areas. This raises the consumption level of poor people who are below the poverty line. Ever since it came in inception, the migration of poor people from rural to urban areas has been checked up to a large extent. The consumption level is the most important part of the contribution to national income and hence growth. If the consumption level is not high, the growth suffers. This programme is similar to Roosevelt's "New Deal" programme of the great depression period of the 1930s. Franklin D. Roosevelt was the wartime US President (1933-45). The whole world was in depression and there was 25% unemployment in the USA. Roosevelt got inspiration from the British economist, John Maynard Keynes from his book, "The Theory of Unemployment, Interest, and Money" (Keynes, 1936) and made several welfare-oriented social and government spending programmes. The New Deal did get millions of Americans back to work. In the context of employment generation in rural areas, the MNREGA was working very efficiently. But After Modi came to power this programme suffered. The fund for the MNREGA has been drastically cut. The fund for this financial year 2023-24 has been reduced from ₹72000 crore to ₹60000 crore which is a cut of 21.66% (Sharma, 2023). MNREGA has been a safeguard against unemployment and inflation. This cut would mean 20 days of work against the entitlement of 100 days for 10 crore of registered wage earners. Actually, there are 17 crore of people who are registered for 100 days of work. The cut of funds of ₹12000 crore would deprive 7 crores of people out of work. This would mean that 10 crore active job card holders would get jobs of only 20 days. As per the growing population we need ₹ 2.72 lakh crore to provide rural employment to job card holders. Unfortunately, the linking of Aadhar with Job Card has put 50% of workers ineligible for MNREGA beneficiaries (Nihalani, 2023). All this shows the apathy of this government for the rural people. None of the welfare programmes launched by the Modi regime is a better or good substitute for MNREGA. Therefore, the present government should consider MNREGA on merit and try to remove existing lacunae for the success of this scheme.

Actually, in the UPA-II government, the centre enacted NFSA (National Food Security Act) in July 2013 which gave legal entitlement to 67% of the population (75% in rural areas and 50% in urban areas) to receive highly subsidized food grain. The coverage of this NFSA is based on 2011 census data. This was later changed to PM-GKAY (Prime Minister Garib Kalyan Anna Yojana) in April 2020 in order to help the poor people whose livelihoods were shuttered by a countrywide lockdown aimed at checking the spread of Covid-19. Under this scheme, about 80 crore beneficiaries covered under the NFSA would get 5kg of food grains per person per month free of cost (Shankar, 2022). This is in addition to the subsidized food grains that come under NFSA. So far ₹ 3.45 lakh crore since 2020 has been incurred. There is an end to this PMGKAY in 2023. Free rationing to the poor and poorest among the poor free of cost has been most helpful to the marginal wage earners when there has been a slump in employment, and the government public expenditure programme is limited now. The government has not looked for alternative means to generate employment for the rural and urban poor for raising the consumption level which in turn would lead to growth and development.

******

Curtailment of Power of Judiciary

For a powerful democracy, it is essential that there should be well- defined separation of power among the legislature, executive, and judiciary. Each one of them puts a check on others so that democracy is strengthened and becomes more powerful to give equity and social justice to the common man. Although, there have been attempts of encroachments by the executive on the power of the judiciary by the erstwhile governments before 2014. But ever since Modi came into power in 2014 we find that there are constant attempts at encroachment of the Supreme Court, which is the supreme authority of justice by our constitution. The Chief Justices are criticized to have given politically sensitive cases to select benches to give favour to the executive and rich people at the detriment of justice to the common man. In politically sensitive matters, the Supreme Court has disappointed us. In an interview with Karan Thapar on Wire, retired Chief Justice of Delhi and Madras High Court, and also Chairman of Law Commission Justice Ajit Prakash Shah is reported to have said that during Modi's regime from 2017 to 2022, the Supreme Court succumbed to the executive (The Wire, 2022). The Chief Justices have not played a positive role. They have more or less succumbed to the executive. According to him, the period of 1993-2013 has been the golden period when the Supreme Court proved its worth in delivering the judgement to the common man. It was after Chief Justice T. S. Thakur, who demitted office in 2017 that things started worsening. The peak was with Chief Justice Ranjan Gogoi who accepted the membership of Rajya Sabha immediately after demitting his office three months after. During this period, the Supreme Court which is regarded as the protector of the constitution of India and custodian of the fundamental rights of citizens has miserably failed. As per the code of conduct of the judiciary, the judges are not supposed to involve themselves in sycophancy. Once they do sycophancy, it is like lowering the independence of the judiciary. In the BJP manifesto, it was clearly stated that judges should not get government jobs after their retirement. Arun Jaitley, the former cabinet minister had emphasized this. But we find that immediately after demitting the office of CJ, Justice P. Sathasivam was appointed as Governor of Kerala. When judges get political appointments, the Supreme Court which is supposed to work as a bulwark to stop the erosion of democracy, fails. It is in this light that the judges should not accept political appointments nor the governments should offer political appointments to retired judges. But in the Modi regime, we find such compromises. We have seen how Justice Arun Mishra praised Modi as a "versatile genius who thinks globally and acts locally (The Hindu, 20th February 2020)." The Supreme Court Bar Association condemned this as improper and unnecessary. Later in January 2021, Justice Mishra was appointed as head of the National Human Rights Commission (NHRC, June 2, 2021). When a sitting judge is full of praise for the executive, can we expect him to be fair in delivering justice to the common man? In Modi's regime, democracy is under seizing as there is no protection of fundamental rights. All opposition leaders are subjected to CBI and ED (Enforcement Directorate) raids regarding the laundering of money when during the last nine years there have been no raids on leaders of BJP. This is a blatant violation of the code of conduct of impartial government machinery (Dushyant Dave, 22nd

October 2022). The Supreme Court's judgement in Justice Loya's case is full of controversy where independent investigation was not allowed. The family of Justice Loya had requested for an independent investigation as Justice Loya had died under suspicious circumstances. In another case, a Hindu girl Hadia who wanted to marry a Muslim boy was not allowed by the Kerala High Court on the pretext of "love jihad" which is deeply regretted. Her father had moved a Writ Petition in the Kerala High Court alleging that her daughter Akhila Ashokan (Hadia) had been misled and forced to become a Muslim. He also alleged that her husband Shafin Jahan had links to extremist Muslim organisations. Hadia maintained throughout the high court proceedings that her conversion to Islam , as well as marriage to Shafin Jahan, was of her own volition. But the Kerala High Court annulled her marriage and called it a 'sham.' The judgement observed that the marriage decision being the most important decision of Hadia, can only be taken with the active involvement of her parents. Thereafter, she was forced to stay with her parents. Later, when Shafin Jahan moved to the Supreme Court, the Supreme Court restored her marriage and her conversion to Islam. But before the judgement was announced, Chief Justice Khehar had taken an extraordinary step of ordering the National Investigation Agency (NIA) to investigate Hadia's marriage which was not at all called for. This is so disgraceful on the part of CJ Khehar to order NIA. Although later in judgement there is no mention of NIA in the court's judgement (Hadia Case, April 9, 2018). Here Justice Chandrachud had expanded the horizon of the right to freedom and observed that the Kerala High Court could not have used Article 226 to annul the marriage of an adult. Thus, where the Supreme Court had almost failed in giving justice to Hadia under Khehar, Justice

Chandrachud gave a landmark judgement on the freedom of marriage by an adult.

Another case of controversy is Jay Shah, the son of Amit Shah, the home minister of the present regime. The Lodha Committee was appointed by the Supreme Court of India on 22 January 2015 for implementable actions for improving the Board of Control for Cricket in India (BCCI). It was also meant to assess the quantum of punishment for Gurunath Meiyappan and Raj Kundra in the Indian Premier League (IPL) betting scandal. On the basis of the Lodha Committee Recommendation, the Supreme Court gave its initial ruling in July 2016, on the case, signalling the end of unethical practices in Indian Cricket like spot-fixing scandal. It also recommended a "cooling off period" of three years for BCCI officers. For Lodha, the cooling-off period was the most important part of his judgement. But later on 14 September 2016, the Supreme Court allowed the BCCI to delete the clause of a "cooling off period" of three years after serving two consecutive three-year terms in either a state association or the BCCI or between them combined. This judgement led to the continuation of Jay Shah and Saurabh Ganguly as Secretary and President of BCCI. This shows the undue influence of the executive over the judiciary. Kundra and Meiyappan were banned from the cricket administration for life.

The executive has always wanted to have its supremacy over the judiciary in the appointment of judges of the High Court and Supreme Court. At the moment, there is a "Collegium" to appoint the judges. The Chief Justice of India along with four senior most judges appoints the judges of the Supreme Court. This collegium also has the power to transfer of judges. For the high court, this collegium has the Chief Justice of the High Court and two senior-most judges who have the power to appoint and transfer the judges of the high court. These recommendations are sent to the government for approval which the government does. Thereafter, the list is sent to the president for final appointment. The government can examine the cases and suggest for amendments, but ultimately it is CJ's word that counts.

Ever since Modi government came into power, the government wanted to have control over the appointment of judges. But such efforts have been thwarted by different successive benches of the Supreme Court. The last was in 2015 when a five-judge Constitution Bench turned down the constitutional amendment act that sought to create the NJAC (National Judicial Appointments Commission) which was swiftly cleared by the Narendra Modi government. Thus the bench sealed the fate of the proposed system that held that the appointment of judges shall continue to be made by the collegium, in which the CJI will have "the last word."

Former Law Minister Kiren Rijiju again raised the issue of the role of an executive in the appointment of judges. He has stated that there is a backlog of cases and the judiciary is too slow in the delivery of judgements. Moreover, there is nepotism and favouritism in the appointment of judges by the collegium. Therefore, what he is suggesting is that appointment of judges should be made by the government. He is reported to have stated that half of the time of judges is devoted to decide whom they have to appoint rather than delivering the judgements of pending cases. Ramana (2021) in response to the controversy in the media in 2021 defended the collegium and stated that the collegium is sacrosanct and has dignity attached to it. He holds the freedom of media and the rights of individuals in high esteem. Hence, to criticize the collegium would be counterproductive. Actually, on the contrary, it is the government that delays the processing of recommendations sent by the CJI. In recent times, Ramana and Lalit have done remarkable jobs in streamlining the backlog of cases. There is a need for structural reforms which can be done with the close coordination of the judiciary and executive. But, more often, it is the executive that wanted control over the judiciary. Many innocent people, against whom there are no charges, are in jail. This is due to the failure of the executive over its supervision of police and law and order.

In fact, the government is the real litigant who has inflated the number of cases lying in courts. They did not do any satisfactory job in expediting the appointment of judges at various levels. The delay by the government in expediting the cases of judges may be construed as a deliberate attempt to delay justice and thereby create anarchy in the rule of law established by the Constitution.

In most recent times, we have come across the frank opinion expressed by the retired SC judge V Gopal Gowda at a National Convention on the topic 'Save Constitution, Save Democracy' organised by the All India Lawyers Union, Delhi Union of Journalists, and Democratic Teachers Front that "In 2014, the apex court was not hesitant in going against the central executive in matters involving high political stakes, be it in the cancellation of 2G licenses and the coal gate case." The Court also passed several oral remarks, including the famous "CBI is caged parrot" remark. The judiciary was seen as a crusader against corruption. But post-2014, the Supreme Court presented a weaker self. The verdict in politically charged cases such as Sahara-Birla (where enquiry was sought against PM Narendra Modi), Loya case (where enquiry was sought regarding the death of judge trying the case against Amit Shah), Bhima-Koregan, Rafale, Aadhaar etc., have invited a lot of criticism of the public. When it comes to taking on the system, the Court acts hesitant (Gowda, Gopal 2023). Before 2014, which is when PM Modi rose to power, the Supreme Court was far more likely to hold the govt to the task.

The judiciary is the third most important pillar of democracy. The judiciary is also a bulwark to stop any erosion of the fundamental rights of people. Hence, the collegium system of appointment of judges must not be given to the executive (Indian Express, December 9, 2022).

******

Climate Change and Its Adaptation

Climate change is one of the largest and most complex problems the developing community has ever faced. India is among the most vulnerable countries where the impact of climate change is most on economic activities and lives and livelihoods. Here 400 million people depend upon exploitation of natural resources and on rain for their livelihoods. As the impacts of higher temperatures, variable precipitation, and extreme weather events have already begun to impact the economic performance of countries and the lives and livelihoods of millions of poor people, India is no exception to these impacts (World Bank, 2011).

Climate Change and its Impact on Economic Development have drawn my attention ever since I wrote on "Sustainable development – some key issues" in 'Employment News', New Delhi, 1-7 August 1998 (Sharma, 1998). The goal of sustainable development is to sustain growth at a rate reasonable for our progeny without lowering the standard of living. We emphasised protection of non-renewable resources like coal and fossil fuels. We must concentrate on renewable resources for energy and power. We must also go for lowering down the greenhouse gases. We should go for the protection of the environment by planting trees and protecting the forests. We must believe in meta- economics which emphasizes the production function taking into view the long run prospective of plants and trees rather than mere demand and supply of commodities (Schumacher, 1973). As the development took place by depletion of natural resources, the global temperature started rising which had a devastating impact on the balance of nature resulting into ravages of flood, cyclones and lowering of water levels. This has also resulted into making our lives full of hardships. Without judicious selection or priority, mass extermination and exploitation of natural resources would lead to the depletion of coal, fossil fuels and flora and fauna of forests. As things were not in control and there was a threat of survival of our existence, most of nations agreed that there must be a legally binding accord on climate change and its adaptation. In this direction, the Intergovernmental Panel on Climate Change was established by the World Meteorological Society and the United Nations Environment Programme in 1988, whose mandate is "to provide the world with a clear scientific view on the current state of knowledge in climate change and its potential environmental and socio-economic impacts." Naturally, as a consequence, UNFCCC (United Nations Framework Convention for Climate Change, 1992) came into being which called for lowering down of global temperature by a reduction in greenhouse gases and avoid exploitation of non-renewable resources. The Kyoto Protocol of 1997 extended the UNFCCC of 1992 (Kyoto, 1997). It was founded to address the critical aspects of climate change. It committed member nations to reduce the greenhouse gases which are driving the global temperature. These are Carbon Di Oxide (CO_2), Methane (CH_4), Nitrous Oxide (N_2O), Hydrofluorocarbons (HFCs), Perfluorocarbons (PFCs), and Sulphur hexafluoride (SF_6). Of all these, CO_2 contributes most in raising the global temperature. Since Kyoto Protocol was also limited to commitments by the member countries to address the critical areas of climate change, there was need of a legally binding treaty by member nations to take vows.

Naturally, a legally binding treaty was made in Paris in December 2015 in which 196 countries participated. They vowed to protect the climate and adapt to its changes. Before the pre-industrial era, the global temperature was almost equal to zero degrees Celsius. In the industrial era the temperature grew to 1.5 degree Celsius. Now, the global temperature is more than 2 degree Celsius. The climate change and its adaptation to bring out policy reforms for stabilizing the rise of global temperature below 1.5 degree Celsius must be given top priority by all nations. It must also be consistent with a consensus to lower down greenhouse gas emissions for climate-resilient development. To make this happen in the near future, we need excellent cooperation and coordination to pursue the goals of the Paris Climate Accord by most participating countries (Paris Climate Accord, 2015). Although we have had remarkable success in adaptation to climate change, but there are many countries which have reversed the trend from low-carbon solutions to fossil fuels in recent Covid-19 pandemic for reversal of unemployment in their countries. Such a trend will ultimately lead to disasters in the long turn.

China, the US, and India are the leading greenhouse gas emitters. The US has re-joined the Paris Accord with Joe Biden taking charge of the Presidency in the USA. China and India have also promised to lower green gas emissions for climate adaptation. But with the Covid-19 pandemic, we find the reversal of trends for job security and development. The countries may be conscious of their development agenda, but climate change must be addressed. In fact, 'climate change and its adaptation' is inextricably related to the protection of lives and livelihoods. In India, during the last nine years of wrong policy measures of demonetization, Goods Service Tax, inflating NPA, and monetary and fiscal policy, India has suffered the most. The Covid-19 pandemic also complicated the whole process of development. After the Covid-19 pandemic, due to a shortage of jobs and the demand of more energy requirements than green energy production, India has bounced back to 'low greenhouse gas emissions.' This is also owing to continuing shift towards wealthy, urban living and crony capitalism. As China and India constitute 36 per cent of the world's population, their development towards low-carbon solutions would pave the way for sustainable development not only for these two countries but for the whole world. Areas of cooperation and coordination in alternate energy development among the member partners of the Paris Accord, is most desirable. Coal being the main source of energy, India is the third largest emitter of the greenhouse gases in the world (Carbon Brief, 2019). By checking the greenhouse gas emissions (which lead to air pollution) would help improve the health status of people. It has been estimated that such measures would be cost-effective.

In 2019 China is estimated to have emitted 27% of world GHG, followed by the US with 11%, then India with 6.6% (BBC, 7/05/2021). As of September 2021, India generates 39.8% of its electricity from renewable energy sources and 60.2% of its electricity from fossil fuels of which 51% is generated from coal. As well as coal mining in India, the country also imports coal to burn in coal-fired power stations in India. New plants are unlikely to be built, old and dirty plants may be shut down and more coal may be burnt in the remaining plants. India is also the world no. 2 buyer of coal. This is essentially required for the installation of new plants when old and redundant coal plants would be shut down in the near future. At COP26 at Glasgow, India promised to have net zero by 2070, a date two decades far behind many countries. This is a very important announcement by Modi at the international forum that would bind him to act likewise. But Modi most often is non-committal in his promises. Even China has net-zero targets by 2060. India has also targeted 2030 as the year of energy production of 500GW without the use of fossil fuels. India also wishes to lower the carbon intensity of energy by 45% by 2030. She also promises to draw half of its energy requirement from renewable sources by 2030 and cut 1 billion tons of GHG emissions from the amount projected by the year 2030.

As per commitment to Paris Accord, India has to submit its biennial transparency report in 2024 to UNFCCC. During the last nine years, we have seen the devastating impact of climate change on water resources (excessive rainwater leading to floods), rise in temperature leading to low productivity in agriculture, rise in GHG leading to health hazards due to air pollution, rising sea levels leading to drowning of coastal areas, severe economic impact leading to migration of people, and a mix of deforestation and changes in land use. We have found that almost all States and Union Territories are the victims of climate change. Even after so much devastation, we have not learned lessons from the fury of nature due to global warming. It has been found that by switching over to net-zero GHG the rise of employment generation is much more than the conventional means of energy production. In 2008, when there was a UPA-I government at the centre, India published its National Action Plan on Climate Change (NAPCC) and India set its goal of 6% of its total energy mix by renewable resources by 2022.

The latest conference was COP27 which was held in Sharm El Sheikh of Egypt from 6th November to 18th November 2022 and is full of challenges to member countries. Among others, the most important challenge is funding to countries who are vulnerable due to catastrophes of climate change, viz. floods, dispersal of people, etc. and compensation to countries who are adopting the non-conventional means of production of energy to meet their national requirements (David Leval, Nov. 2022). How do we support transformational change in regions and communities whose revenue sources will shrink as the climate changes? A process at COP 27 aims to double funding for adaptation and resilience to more than $40 billion by 2025, but it is still unclear where this enormous pool of money will come from. A major issue is how to encourage the private sector to fund adaptation actions that do not produce an immediate return on investments, such as helping farmers transition from an at-risk activity to more resilient practices.

How will the traditional financial institutions that were established post second world war cater to the new challenges of climate change and adaptation? India is one of the four hotspots countries of the world which is prone to climate change. National Action Plan on Climate Change (NAPCC) is the major climate action plan in India, which has eight sub-plans. These eight sub-plans are represented by different missions namely

1. National Solar Mission; 2. National Mission for Enhanced Energy Efficiency; 3. National Mission on Sustainable Habitat; 4. National Water Mission; 5. National Mission for Sustaining the Himalayan Ecosystem; 6. National Mission for a Green India; 7. National Mission for Sustainable Agriculture; and 8. National Mission on Strategic Knowledge for Climate Change. Each mission is under a different ministry due to which the issue of climate change and its impact is not properly addressed. The IPCC recommendations emphasized achieving the goal of net zero emission of carbon by 2050

and taking care on impacts of climate change on coastal, ocean, polar and mountain ecosystems, as well as the impacts on the human communities that depend on these ecosystems. Similar to most countries, despite the measures to tackle climate change, India is going to fall short of the IPCC recommendations unless the policies take up all development goals and focus solely on climate change. India must have a dedicated ministry of Climate Change and its adaptation to take corrective measures. The UN financing to decimate the impact of climate change must also be a part of this new ministry. Since the NAPCC of 2008, India does not have any other concerted plan for climate change.

Although all country's goal is to have high growth for more productivity and employment generation; we must remember that the goal of high growth will lead to more exploitation of our fossil fuel, coal and natural resources than their substitution. Hence, there should be a low growth target, but the emphasis should be on the adoption of environmentally friendly technologies which are more employment-generating. Hence, we should go for low growth but sustainable development considering the futuristic outlook of climate change due to global warming. We should concentrate on net zero carbon emission in all our production methods. We should also concentrate on the health status of the common man as climate change brings adverse catastrophe on people living in coastal areas where it seriously affects their lives and livelihoods. One most important issue should be a change of traditional methods to non-conventional methods of energy generation. Another most important issue should be rainwater harvesting.

So far, India does not have long-term planning for a comprehensive concerted action on climate change. It appears that she has been doing only lip services so far just to be a member of COP of UNFCCC. Simply proposing targets of reduction of GHG by 2030 or net Zero by 2070 will not help us. Rather climate change and its impact will derail our economy from long-term development to severe backwardness and other health-related ailments.

The most condemnable part of the Modi government is the recent finding of the Washington Post (2022) that there is a secret pact between India and Bangladesh in which business tycoon Gautam Adani has got undue favour of raising a thermal project in Godda of Jharkhand to supply power to Bangladesh without any tax to be paid by Adani (Shih, Masih and Gupta, 2022). Only Adani would get a return at the cost of severe pollution and health hazard to the people at Godda. Our natural resources are also going to be depleted. Whereas the whole world is discouraging the use of coal in the generation of energy, India is encouraging Adani at a massively large scale. This very much goes against the promises Modi made at COP26 to achieve a net-zero target by 2070.

Adani is a friend of Modi and hence Adani can never go against the will of Modi. Godda Super Thermal Power Plant by Adani would not have started without the consent of Modi. If Modi is interested in 'climate change and its adaptation', and also interested in reduction of GHG, the climate hazard of Godda would have never come. Naturally, such efforts lower down our prestige among the comity of nations who are committed to fighting against GHG.

Modi must hold a meeting of all States and Union Territories to take measures to reduce GHG and help financially for the adoption of climate change. Although some efforts have been made to make people aware of the adoption of non-conventional methods of generation of power but it is sorry to say that most of the government offices do not have solar power plants and rainwater harvesting. The government does not have a rigorous plan of the installation of solar power plants on the rooftops of houses. The government does not have a coordinated plan for giving incentives to people. All municipalities and gram Panchayats must give instructions to households for rainwater harvesting. All multi-flats and hotels that draw water from the ground by submersible motors should have downpipes going down the earth for restoring the rainwater on their rooftops. This would check the groundwater depletion. All houses must also have some open areas for plantation. Once the level of groundwater is maintained by installing downpipes from the roof and letting it go to the underground pit, we would not face the problem of water scarcity in summer. Since the government has not thought out of a concrete plan the rainwater is wasted and it flows to the river and then to the ocean. Finally, when the ocean water is evaporated due to the sun's rays, it goes into the air which later when condenses falls in the form of rain. Since the overflow of rainwater is excessive, the water vapour from the ocean is also excessive which results in heavy rainfall. This leads to flood and other kinds of misery for the people. Hence, the government must take this to the grass root level to economise the use of water and also restore the excess rain water for maintaining the level of groundwater. The Municipalities and Nagar Nigams must not approve the building plan of any house if there is no provision of rainwater harvesting in it.

Just to summarise the COP27, there are five takeaways which are most relevant now if we wish to achieve the target of net zero GHG by 2030 according to

UN Secretary-General António Guterres (UNFCCC, 2023). These five cardinal points are (i) the Establishment of a dedicated fund for loss and damage for adapting the climate change, (ii) Maintaining a clear intention to keep 1.5 degrees Celsius within reach, (iii) Holding businesses and institutions to account, (iv) Mobilizing more financial support for developing countries, and (v) Making the pivot toward implementation. The most important point is making the pivot toward the implementation of promises. The other most important point is a dedicated fund for compensating the loss and damages caused due to the adoption of means to achieve the target. India being a leading country among developing countries, she must have a forward-looking policy. Once, the government decides to implement the promises we would find that there are many grey areas within and outside India. How we are going to cope up the challenges depends upon how our government coordinates with multilateral organisations to obtain the objective of climate change and its adaptation? Naturally, Modi should rise above narrow parochialism and treat all States equally for mitigating the ravages done by nature's furies and also adopt a uniform policy for the production of green energy.

Modi regards 'climate change' as a hoax. Before his becoming the PM of India in 2014, he supported Al Gore, the US Vice President who is famous for environmental protection from global warming. In his apparent tribute to Al Gore in his e-book in 2011 called Convenient Action frames action on climate change as a moral duty. During that time Modi was the CM of Gujarat.

But later on, 5th September 2014 when he was the PM, addressed the gathering of teachers and students in Bangalore from Delhi. In his live telecast, he stated that the climate has not changed, rather we have changed. He was also vague on global warming and he did not know how it is caused (Goldenberg, 2014). It is really very shameful for us when we find that our leader is ignorant of climate change. It appears that even the PM's men are not aware of the challenges the 'climate change and its adaptation' has put before us. Modi who is unaware of the science behind climate change may be excused, but his bureaucrats can never be forgiven for such an important issue.

Now that nine years have passed and there have been many conferences on climate change, we are sure Modi and his officials would take climate change as a very important issue of development.

******

References

Anand, Nupur (2018) 'Everything you need to know about the massive crisis brewing in India's financial markets', *Quartz India*, September 25, 2018, retrieved from https://qz.com/india/1401032/why-the-ilfs-default-is-spooking-india/

Ananthakrishnan G. (2022) *SC to Govt: Show us EC Arun Goel's appointment file, if no hanky panky, don't fear.* The bench said it wanted to know the mechanism that was followed. It asked the government to produce the file on Thursday when it will hear the matter again. Available at: https://indianexpress.com/article/india/supreme-court-election-commissioner-arun-goel-appointment-8285549/ dated November 24, 2022.

Bajpayee (2004) *Address to seek vote of Confidence in Parliament in 2004.*

BBC (2017) *Gauri Lankesh: Indian journalist shot dead in Bangalore,* Available at: https://www.bbc.com/news/world-asia-india-41169817, dated 6th September, 2017. In the last few years, journalists seen to be critical of Hindu nationalists have been berated on social media, while many women reporters have been threatened with rape and assault. Ministers belonging to India's ruling Bhartiya Janata Party (BJP) have also openly attacked journalists, using terms like "presstitute" (a mix of press and prostitute) to describe them.

BBC (2018) *India's top court has backed Delhi's government in a battle with the central government over who runs the capital*, Available at: https://www.bbc.com/news/world-asia-india-44708633, July 4, 2018

BBC Hindi (1996) *Atal Bihari Bajpayee's Best Speech in Parliament in 1996.*

BBC News (2021-05-07) *Report: China emissions exceed all developed nations combined.*

Bismee, Taskin (2021) *4 journalists 'murdered' in India for their work in 2021, most in world, says media watchdog*, Available at: https://theprint.in/india/4-journalists-murdered-in-india-for-their-work-in-2021-most-in-world-says-media-watchdog/779388/

BJP (2019) *Establishment of Hindu Rashtra: Manifesto of 2019.*

Bloomberg.com (August 2019) *India, World's No. 2 Coal Buyer, Plans to Cut Imports by a Third.* (Accessed: September 27, 2019).

Bommai, S. R. vs. Union of India, 1994.

Business Standard (2022) *India Covid death toll highest in world, says WHO as govt.* Available at: https://www.business-standard.com/article/current-affairs/4-7-mn-died-of-covid-in-india-ten-times-more-than-govt-figure-who-122050501193_1.html, dated May 06 2022.

Business Today (2021) *BJP received over ₹ 750 corer from corporate, individual* ...Available at: https://www.businesstoday.in › ... › Economy Politics, Jun 10, 2021

Carbon Brief (2019-03-14) *the Carbon Brief Profile: India* (Accessed: November 05, 2022).

Census (2011) *Census Report 2011*, Available at: https://www.census2011.co.in.

Centre for creative leadership. *Leadership Development Program*, ccl.org, 1, Place, Greensboro, NC 27410, USA

Chen, James. (2022) *Understanding Antitrust-laws*, updated May 02, 2022 Available at: https://www.investopedia.com/ask/answers/09/antitrust-law.asp

Chopra, Ritika. (2021) *5 ex-CECs weigh in: Government note to EC unacceptable, interaction with PMO undermines poll panel* Available at: https://indianexpress.com/article/india/pm-cant-call-meeting-cec-7677667/ (Accessed: December 17, 2021.

Congressional Research Service (2023*) India: Human Rights Assessments*, Available at: https://crsreports.congress.gov, dated July 5, 2023.

CPI (M) WB WebDesk (2022) *Indianness In The Constitution Of India And Assault Of The RSS*, Available at: https://cpimwb.org.in/en/indianness-in-the-constitution-of-india-and-assault-of-the-rss/ dated

CPJ, *Committee to Protect Journalists* - www.cpj.org

Dave, Dushyant. (2022) *Dissents in Politically Sensitive Matters Justice Chandra Chud Sometimes Disappoints.* Available at: U Tube in interview with Karan Thapar, October 22, 2022

David Leval, (Nov. 2022) *Climate-finance-how-it-affects-our-planets-future* Available at: https://unfoundation.org/blog/post/cop-27-qa- /

Deccan Chronicle (2023) *Five names recommended by Collegium for SC judgeship to be cleared soon: Centre*, Available at:

https://www.deccanchronicle.com/nation/in-other-news/030223/five-names-recommended-by-collegium-for-sc-judgeship-to-be-cleared-soo.html, dated February 3, 2023

Deccan Herald (2022) *BJP MLA demands withdrawal of voting rights of Muslim* .Available at: https://www.deccanherald.com/national/bjp-mla-demands-withdrawal-of-voting-rights-of-muslim-community-1084771.html, dated Feb 24, 2022.

Department of Economic Affairs (2015) *Press Release Introduction of the Scheme of Electoral Bond* Available at: https://dea.gov.in › sites › default › files › Elect...

Duttatreya, Hosabale, RSS Gen Secretary, 1/10/2022

Genocide Watch (1999) institution built up in 1999, 'Abetment to Genocide by Modi & his party.'

Goldenberg, Suzanne. (2014) 'Is Narendra Modi a climate sceptic'?

Gowda, Gopala (2023) *Former SC Judges paint a grim picture of Judiciary with their misplaced, misdirected political rants,* Available at: https://www.opindia.com/2023/01/former-judges-gopala-gowda-judiciary-misdirected-misplaced-political-rants/ ᵗ January 9, 2023

Hadia Case (2018) *Judgment in Plain English - Supreme Court Observer, Supreme* Court Delivered Judgement on 9th April, 2018 Available at: https://www.scobserver.in › reports › shafin-jahan-uni...

Hindenburg (2023) Available at: https://hindenburgresearch.com/adani/

Hindustan Times (2017) *Prime Minister Narendra Modi promised ₹ 10,000 crore and autonomy to 20 universities — 10 public and private — in the country so as to compete globally and be counted among the world's best institutions,* Available at: https://www.hindustantimes.com/india-news/pm-modi-in-patna-20-universities-to-get-rs-10-000-crore-over-5-years-for-world-class-education-system/story-ITrXDsWL2jCo1kkQtwRgoN.html, dated Oct 14, 2017.

Hindustan Times (2022) *Around 3400 communal riots took place from 2016-2020, Available at:* https://www.hindustantimes.com/india-news/around-3-400-communal-riots-took-place-from-2016-2020-centre-101648611989880.html, dated March 30, 2022.

HRP Report (2022) *Country Reports on Human Rights Practices: India*, Available at https://www.state.gov/reports/2022-country-reports-on-human-rights-practices/india#:~:text=According%20to%20the%20Human%20Rights,a%20wide%20variety%20of%20views

https://en.wikipedia.org/wiki/Hadiya_case.

https://en.wikipedia.org/wiki/Hindu nationalism.

https://indianexpress.com/article/explained/debate-over-the-collegium-system-how-are-sc-and-hc-judges-appointed-8158195/ Oct 08, 2022.

https://powermin.gov.in/en/content/power-sector-glance-all-india. 11/08/2022.

https://timesofindia.indiatimes.com/india/87-former-bureaucrats-police-officers-write-open-letter-on-blatant-violation-of-rule-of-law-in-uttar-pradesh, Jul-12, 2021.

https://www.deccanchronicle.com/opinion/columnists/290919/is-constitution-anti-hindu-or-the-rss-anti-indian.html, September 29, 2019.

https://www.imf.org/en/News/Articles/2021/11/02/na111121-indias-economy-to-rebound-as-pandemic-prompts-reforms.

https://www.thehindu.com/news/cities/Delhi/centre-notifies-gnct-act-that-gives-more-powers-to-delhi-l-g/article34428245.ece, April 28, 2021.

https://www.thehindu.com/news/national/certain-sections-of-media-communalise-everything-says-cji/article36243837.ece.

https://www.tni.org/my/node/24669 (on Hindu Rashtra).

Human Rights Violations: *A Curse to Society, Culture and Humanity*, Bhaswat Prakash.

IMF (2021) World Economic Outlook - *International Monetary Fund*, Available at: https://www.imf.org › Publications › WEO, dated November 12, 2021.

India times (2022) *ED raids jumped 27 times during 2014-2022 compared to ...* Available at: https://timesofindia.indiatimes.com › India News

India Today, *JNU row: Did a fake video fuel the anti-national fire?* Available at: https://www.indiatoday.in › India, Feb 18, 2016

India's PM used to call climate action a moral duty, now he tells students 'climate has not changed, we have changed'. Available at: https://www.theguardian.com/environment/2014/sep/09/narendra-modi-india-prime-minister-climate-change-sceptic, Tue Sep 09, 2014 07.09 BST

Indian Express (2023) *The Supreme Court said that hate speech was a serious offence that is capable of affecting the secular fabric of country*, Available at:

https://indianexpress.com/article/india/file-cases-against-hate-speech-supreme-court-to-states-8581381/, dated April 29, 2023.

IPCC Recommendations (2018) Available at: https://unfoundation.org/blog/post/intergovernmental-panel-climate-change-30-years-informing-global-climate-action/?gclid=CjwKCAiAvK2bBhB8EiwAZUbP1ADZXFI October 2018.

Jaffrelot, Christoffe. (2021) *Modi's India: Hindu Nationalism and the Rise of Ethnic Democracy*, Princeton University Press, Princeton, 2021.

Janardhanan, Arun. (2023) *TN Governor relents as Assembly ups ante on pending Bills, passes resolution asking Centre to fix timeframe*, Available at: https://indianexpress.com/article/political-pulse/tamil-nadu-assembly-slams-governor-ravi-resolution-demands-action-tensions-bills-8548196/ dated April 11, 2023.

Jinoy, J. P. (2019) *Resignations in the IAS. What is troubling India's elite officers?* The Hindu, Available at: https://www.thehindubusinessline.com/blink/know/resignations-in-the-ias-what-istroubling-indias-elite-officers/article29528239.ece. (Accessed: September 27, 2019).

Julien, Bouissou. (2022) *In India, 'crony capitalism' is on the rise* Available at: https://www.lemonde.fr/en/opinion/article/2022/09/15/in-india-crony-capitalism-is-on-the-rise_5996996_23.html: (Accessed: October 17, 2022

Kattakayam, Jiby J. (2018) *The withdrawal of criminal cases against politicians by UP*, Available at: https://timesofindia.indiatimes.com › jibber-jabber › the ..., January 24, 2018

Katzu, Justice (2021) face book, June 27, 2021.

Keynes, J. M. (1936) *The General Theory of Employment, Interest, and Money.* Available at: https://www.goodreads.com/book/show/303615.The_General_Theory_of_Employment_Interest_and_Money.

Khan, Khadiza (2023) *Govt's power to promulgate, repromulgate Ordinances — why and how,* Available at: https://indianexpress.com/article/explained/explained-law/govts-power-to-promulgate-repromulgate-ordinances-why-how-8625383/, dated May 25, 2023

Kyoto Protocol (1997) Available at: https://unfccc.int/process-and-meetings/the-kyoto-protocol/what-is-the-kyoto-protocol/kyoto-protocol-targets-for-the-first-commitment-period.

Lancet Study (2021) *India reports the highest number of suicide deaths in the world.* The latest study is based on statistics from the National Crime Records Bureau (NCRB). It is noted that the burden of deaths by suicide has increased in India — by 7.2 per cent from 2020 — with a total of 1, 64,033 people dying by suicide in 2021. NCRB, which collects data from police recorded suicide cases, further stipulates in Chapter-2 of the report that every year, more than 1, 00,000 people die by suicide in the country. The report follows a 2021 Lancet study that noted. Available at: https://indianexpress.com/article/lifestyle/health/ncrb-report-2021-death-by-suicide-rate-increase-mental-health-experts-realistic-ti

Lewitsky, S. and Ziblatt, D. (2018) *How Democracies die, London,* Penguin Random House, UK.

Lincoln, Abraham (1809-65) 16th US President.

Lodha Committee (2015) Available at: https://en.wikipedia.org › wiki › Lodha Committee, July 14, 2015.

Machiavelli, Niccolo (1513) *Machiavellianism is characterized by manipulation and exploitation of others, an absence of morality, unemotional callousness, and a higher level of self-interest.*

Machiavelli, Niccolo (1513) *The Prince.*

Mathur, Aneesha (2021) *Recently, the CJI Supreme Court is reported to have given his observation that the central investigation agencies like the Enforcement Directorate, the CBI, and NIA keep the cases in suspension.* They delay the charge sheet and linger the cases at the behest of the ruling party at the centre. Available at: https://www.indiatoday.in/law/story/file-chargesheets-keep-hanging-cji-ramana-ed-cbi-delay-cases-mp-mlas-1845054-2021-08-25, dated Aug 25, 2021

Ministry of Finance (2019) *As per RBI provisional data on global operations, as on 31.3.2019, the aggregate amount of gross NPAs of PSBs and Scheduled Commercial Banks (SCBs) were ₹ 8,06,412 crore and ₹ 9,49,279 crore respectively.* Available at: https://pib.gov.in/newsite/PrintRelease.aspx?relid=190704, dated June 24, 2019.

Mishra, Arun (February 2020) available at https://thewire.in/government/controversial-judge-who-praised-modi-to-be-nhrc-chief-opposition-leader-https://www.youtube.com/watch?v=9q-CaW9qaMU; (Accessed: October 26, 2022)

Moneylife Digital Team (2022) 'Jan Dhan Yojana: Nearly 18% or 81.38mn Bank Accounts Are Inoperative, Says Govt' Available at: https://www.moneylife.in/article/jan-dhan-yojana-nearly-18-percentage-or-8138mn-bank-accounts-are-inoperative-says-govt/67969.html, dated August 04, 2022.

MoSPI (2019) *Ministry of Statistics and Programme Implementation Unit Level Data of Periodic Labour Force Survey (PLFS), July 2019.*

MoSPI (2020) *Ministry of Statistics and Programme Implementation* released the GDP figures for Q1 (April to June) FY21, which showed a contraction of 24% as compared to the same period the year before, September 1, 2020.

Mudgil, Amit (2018) *Since 1991, Budget size grew 19 times, economy 9 times,* Feb 19, 2018, Available at: https://economictimes.indiatimes.com/markets/stocks/news/since-1991-budget-size-grew-19-times-economy-9-times-your-income-5-times/articleshow/62735382.cms?from=mdr

Mukunth, Vasudevan (2021) Available at: https://thewire.in/government/this-august-15-lets-swallow-the-modicine-and-declare-our-independence-from-science. 04-Aug-2021 (Accessed: August 7, 2021).

National Action Plan on Climate Change, 2008.

National Sample Survey Office (2014) *Employment and Unemployment Situation in India, NSS 68th round, (July 2011- June 2012).* Ministry of Statistics and Programme Implementation, Available at: http://mospi.nic.in/sites/default/files/publication_reports/nss_report_554_31jan14.pdf, January 2014,

National Statistical Organisation (2022) PRESS NOTE ON SECOND ADVANCE ESTIMATES OF NATIONAL INCOME 2022-23, QUARTERLY ESTIMATES OF GROSS DOMESTIC PRODUCT FOR THE THIRD QUARTER (Q3) OF 2022-23 AND

FIRST REVISED ESTIMATES OF NATIONAL INCOME, CONSUMPTION EXPENDITURE, SAVING AND CAPITAL FORMATION FOR 2021-22, Available at: https://www.mospi.gov.in › files › press release, dated May 31, 2022.

NCRB (2019) *National Crime Records Bureau*, 2019

NCRB (2021) *Accidental Deaths and Suicides in India (ADSI) Report 2021* Available at: https://economictimes.indiatimes.com/news/india/over-17000-farmers-committed-suicide-in-3-years-govt-in-lok-sabha/articleshow/89433112.cms, February 8, 2022

NDTV (2021) *Testing Our Patience: Supreme Court Ultimatum to Centre*, Available at: https://www.ndtv.com › India News, September 6, 2021

NDTV, *PM Modi's address in a rally of West Bengal General election.* U Tube,

Nehru, J L, *Discovery of India*, Kindle Store.

Nehru, JL (1947) *Tryst with Destiny: Independence Day Speech, 1947.*

NHRC (2021) *Mr. Justice Arun Kumar Mishra, former Judge of the Supreme appointed as Chairman of NHRC*, Available at: https://nhrc.nic.in › media › press-release › mr-justice-a..., Jun 2, 2021

Nihalani, J. (2023) 'In 14 states, more than 50% of workers are not eligible for the Adhar based payment system', *The Hindu*, Feb 27, 2023, Lucknow.

NOMOS (2000) *Designing Democratic Institutions: NOMOS XLII* (NOMOS- American Society for Political and Legal Philosophy, 32).

Noorani, A. G (2019) *Is Constitution 'anti-Hindu' or the RSS anti-Indian?* Available at:

https://www.deccanchronicle.com/opinion/columnists/290919/is-constitution-anti-hindu-or-the-rss-anti-indian.html, Sept. 29, 2019.

Outlook (2023) *The "basic structure" doctrine was evolved in order to prevent a majoritarian-driven assault on the foundational principles of the Constitution, the former Union minister Chidambaram had said*, Available at: https://www.outlookindia.com/national/congress-slams-vp-dhankar-cites-venkaiyah-naidu-s-2020-constitution-is-supreme-remarks-news-253254, dated Jan 13, 2023.

Panagariya (2017) *UN Seventeen Development Goal Available at:* https://sdgs.un.org/goals, visited 23 March, 2023.

Panchayati Raj Constitutional Amendment Act of 1992 (73rd Amendment).

Paris Accord (2015) Available at: https://unfccc.int/process-and-meetings/the-paris-agreement/the-paris-agreement?gclid=Cj0KCQjwqc6aBhC4ARIsAN06NmPo8MFMUikabn0, (Accessed: October 22, 2022).

PMINDIA (2024) Available at: https://www.pmindia.gov.in/en/governance-track-record/

PM Modi (2017) *If a kabristan can be constructed, a shamshaan too should be built,* Available at: https://www.hindustantimes.com/assembly-elections/if-a-kabristan-can-be-constructed-so-should-a-shamshaan-pm-modi/story-obPfbdpUwPZm98wBKdZmTN.html, 20/02/2017.

Raj, K.N. *Hindu_rate_of_growth* Available at: https://en.wikipedia.or g/wiki/

RAJAGOPAL KRISHNADAS (2023) *What matters is that this is just simply unacceptable… This is the grossest of constitutional and human rights violations… We are expressing our deep concern… We will give the government a little time to take action or we will take action*, the Chief Justice warned. Available at: https://epaper.thehindu.com/ccidist-ws/th/th_delhi/issues/44437/OPS/G6SBGRT6D.1+GBCBGSHTV.1.html, dated July 21, 2023.

Rajagopal, Krishnadas. (2021) *CJI flags 'communal content' in media*, Chief Justice of India N.V. Ramana says ultimately country will get a bad name, Available at: https://www.thehindu.com/news/national/certain-sections-of-media-communalise-everything-says-cji/article36243837.ece, dated September 02, 2021

Rajagopal, Krishnadas. (2021) the hindu.com. August 25, 2021.

Ramana, NV. (2021) *Extremely-upset-with-media-reports*, Available at: https://www.outlookindia.com/website/story/india-news-extremely-upset-with-media-reports-speculating-collegium-recommendations-cji-ramana/391860?utm_source=related_story. August 18, 2021

Rangan, Kasturi. (2020) *Report on New Higher Education Policy.*

Reston, Maeve (2021) *Speaking out against hate crimes, Biden tries to restore moral clarity to the presidency – CNN Politics*, Maeve Reston, CNN, March 20, 2021, Available at: https://www.cnn.com › 2021/03/20 › politics › joe-biden-.

Roth, Kenneth, *World Report 2021* - Human Rights Watch Available at: https://www.hrw.org › world-report › 2021.

RSF (2021) Available at: https://rsf.org/en/2021-world-press-freedom-index-journalism-vaccine-against-disinformation-blocked-more-130-countries.

RSF (2023) 2023 *World Press Freedom Index – journalism threatened by fake content industry*, Available at: https://rsf.org/en/2023-world-press-freedom-index-journalism-threatened-fake-content-industry.

Sampedro, J., Smith, S. J., Arto, I., González-Eguino, M., Markandya, A., Mulvaney, K. M., Pizarro-Irizar, C., & Van Dingenen, R. (2020). Health co-benefits and mitigation costs as per the Paris Agreement under different technological pathways for energy supply. Environment International, 136, 105513. https://doi.org/10.1016/j.envint.2020.105513 (Accessed: January 24, 2023).

Satyahindi.com/ India-Delhi-court, 7/4/2022).

SC Bar Association (2020) *Condemns Justice Mishra's open praise of Modi* Available at: https://www.thehindu.com › News › India; February 26, 2020.

Schumacher, E. F. (1973) *Small is Beautiful*, 1973: "Modern economic systems have brought great prosperity to the Western world; however, that prosperity came with a big price tag. Our lives are now so removed from nature that we constantly destroy it without compunction. For instance, thanks to the global industrial system, we squander a great deal of our precious natural resources – such as fossil fuels. The modern economy treats fossil fuels as income, a constant stream of goods, rather than capital, a finite supply of goods. To thus regard them is a way of justifying waste. If we viewed fossil fuels as capital rather than income we'd be much more concerned with their conservation.

However, we use them as if they'll never run out – which, of course, they will."

Sen, Amartya (2021) Available at: https://timesofindia.indiatimes.com/business/india-business/centres-schizophrenia-led-to-covid-ravages-amartya-sen/articleshow/83253332. Dated June 5, 2021

Sen, Somdeep (2021) Associate Professor of International Development Studies at Roskilde University

Shankar, R. (2022) *'What is Pradhan Mantri Garib Kalyan Anna Yojana?* Available at: https://timesofindia.indiatimes.com/business/faqs/miscellaneous/what-is-pradhan-mantri-garib-kalyan-anna-yojana/articleshow/94699853.cms, dated Oct 7, 2022.

Sharma, S. K. (2019) *Economic Consequences and overall implications of BJP rule during 2014-19 in India*, Available at: https://rpajournals.com/wp-content/uploads/2020/06/ARICON-2019-JIBM-9.pdf.

Sharma, S. K. 'Sustainable development – some key issues.' *Employment News*, New Delhi, 1-7 August, 1998.

Sharma, S.K. and Mishra, D.K. (1982) 'Pricing Policy of Agricultural Commodities in India' in *Yojana*, New Delhi, July 15, 1982.

Sharma, Y. S. (2023) *Budget allocation for MGNREGA scheme sees a sharp decline in Union Budget 2023*, Available at: https://economictimes.indiatimes.com/news/economy/policy/budget-allocation-for-mgnrega-scheme-sees-a-sharp-decline-. Dated Feb 01, 2023.

Shih, G., Masih, N. and Gupta, A. (2022) 'How political will often favors a coal billionaire and his dirty fossil fuel'. *Washington Post (2022)*, Available at: https://www.washingtonpost.com › world › 2022/12/09

Shyam, Ashutosh, (2019), 'India's consumption story losing the plot'. *The Economic times*, Available at: https://economictimes.indiatimes.com/news/economy/indicators/indias-consumption-story-losing-the-plot/articleshow/69210037.cms, May 7, 2019.

Smith, Adam (1776), *An Enquiry into the nature and causes of Wealth of Nations.* W. Strahan and T. Cadell, London, Scotland, Great Britain, March 9, 1776

Sonalli (1994) *S.R Bommai v/s union of India, 1994: the verdict concluded that the power of the President to dismiss a state government is not absolute,* Available at: https://www.legalserviceindia.com/legal/article-6253-s-r-bommai-v-s-union-of-india.html

Srivastava, Nitin (2021) *Tripura: Fear and hope after anti-Muslim violence,* Available at: https://www.google.com/search?q=Srivastava%2C+Nitin%2C+25+November%2C+2021%2C+BBC&oq=Srivastava%2C+Nitin%2C+25+November%2C+2021%2C+BBC&aqs=chrome..69i57j33i160l2.412887366j0j15&sourceid=chrome&ie=UTF-8, dated November 25, 2021.

Srivastava, Nitin (2021) *Tripura: Fear and hope after anti-Muslim violence.* Available at: BBC Newshttps://www.bbc.com › world-asia-india-59398367, November 25, 2021.

Stantin, Gregory (2023) *India Country Report April 2023.* Available at: https://www.genocidewatch.com. It exists to build an international movement to prevent and stop genocide and other form of mass murder.

Supreme Court Ultimatum to Centre, "Testing Our Patience".

Swaminathan, M.S. (2006) *Swaminathan Report: National Commission on Farmers.* Available at:

https://prsindia.org/policy/report-summaries/swaminathan-report-national-commission-farmers (Accessed: February 3, 2023).

Taskin, Bismee (2021) *These 5 journalists were killed in India in 2021. 4 'murdered', 1 died on dangerous assignment,* Watchdog Committee to Protect Journalists says India has highest number of journalists who were killed in 'retribution' for their work this year. The Print tracks the cases, and where they stand. Available at: https://theprint.in/india/these-5-journalists-were-killed-in-india-in-2021-4-murdered-1-died-on-dangerous-assignment/779932/ December 11, 2021

Thapar, Karan (2022) Supreme *Court has succumbed to Executive Control after Modi became PM: Justice Shah,* #thewirenews #chiefjusticeofindia, October 2022.

The Economic Times (2021) *New law leaves Delhi's elected govt toothless, all powers with LG,* Available at: https://economictimes.indiatimes.com/news/politics-and-nation/new-law-leaves-delhis-elected-govt-toothless-all-powers-with-lg/articleshow/82292888.cms?from=mdr, April 28, 2021.

The Economic Times, (2022) *CJI's inclusion will ensure independence in appointment of Chief Election Commissioner: Supreme Court,* Available at: https://economictimes.indiatimes.com/topic/appointment-of- November 24, 2022

The Hindu (2014) *India has second fastest growing services sector,* Available at: https://www.thehindu.com › Business › Budget Jul. 09, 2014

The Hindu (2020) *Modi a versatile genius who thinks globally and acts locally,* Available at: https://www.thehindu.com › News › India, February 22, 2020

The Hindu (2021), *CJI flags 'communal content' in media*, dated September 2, 2021, available at https://www.thehindu.com/news/national/certain-sections-of-media-communalise-everything-says-cji/article36243837.ece?homepage=true

The Hindu (2022) *Although India claims to be of 5 trillion economy, but she is at the lowest on EPI (Environment Protection Index)*, 20/06/22).

The Hindu (2022) *Parliament Winter Session updates*, Available at: https://www.thehindu.com › News › India, December 16, 2022.

The Hindu, epaper.thehindu.com, 17/11/2021.

The Hindustan Times (2023) *India topped global list of internet shutdowns for 5th year in row in 2022*, Available at: https://www.hindustantimes.com/india-news/india-topped-global-list-of-internet-shutdowns-for-5th-year-in-row-in-2022-101677567146942.ht, dated Feb 28, 2023.

The Indian Express (2022) Collegium *system is better than the NJAC*. Available at: https://indianexpress.com › Opinion › Columns, dated Dec. 09, 2022

The Lancet (2020) Available at: https://doi.org/10.1016/S0140-, 6736(21)01052-7 Published May 08, 2020 (Accessed: October 10 2022).

The Lancet (2021) *India's COVID-19 emergency: overarching conclusions belie facts*, Available at: www.thelancet.com, Vol. 397 June 26, 2021.

The U.S. State Department's human rights report on India, 2021 *flags curbs on free speech, civil society*, Available at: https://www.thehindu.com/news/international/us-state-departments-human-rights-report-flags-indias-curbs-on-free-speech-civil-society, dated April 13, 2022.

The Washington Post (2022), *How political will often favours a coal billionaire and his dirty..?* Available at: https://www.washingtonpost.com › world › dated Dec.09, 2022.

The Wire (2020) *Why Journalists Are Worried About The New Media Policy in Jammu and Kashmir?* Available at: https://thewire.in/media/kashmir-new-media-policy-press-freedom June 2, 2020,

The Wire (2021) Available at: https://thewire.in/rights/manipur-activist-journalist-jail-cow-dung-covid, dated July 9, 2021.

The Wire (2022 April 17) Available at: https://thewire.in/communalism/jahangirpuri-communal-violence-jahangirpuri, dated April 17, 22).

The Wire (2022) Available at: (https://thewire.in/communalism/hindutva-leaders-dharma-sansad-muslim-genocide, dated December 22, 2022.

The Wire (2022) *Supreme Court has Succumbed to Executive Control after Modi became PM: Justice Shah | Karan Thapar, Available at:* https://www.youtube.com/watch?v=66A1fFn1qec, dated Oct 20, 2022.

The Wire (2022), *The Uses (and Abuses) of Investigative Agencies* Available at: https://thewire.in › government › cbi-nia-enforcement-... dated Nov.12, 2022

The Wire (2023) *BJP Govt Making Systematic Effort to Change Character of Civil Services, Say Former Officers,* Available at: https://thewire.in/government/bjp-open-letter-civil-services-character, dated May 25, 2023.

Tillin, Louise (2019) *Indian Federalism (Oxford India Short Introductions Series).* Dated May 4, 2019.

Times Now, U Tube, *PM Modi's Interview with Arnab Goswami, Private TV Channel Director*, dated June 27, 2016.

Timesnews.com, Feb 26, 2022.

UN (1948), *Universal Declaration of Human rights, 10 December, 1948*, Available at: https://humanrights.gov.au/our-work/what-universal-declaration-human-rights#

UNFCCC (!992) United *Nations Climate Change - The UNFCCC Secretariat*, Available at: https://unfccc.int/process-and-meetings/the-paris-agreement

UNFCCC (2023) *Five Key Takeaways from COP27*, Available at: https://unfccc.int/process-and-meetings/conferences/sharm-el-sheikh-climate-change-conference-november-2022/five-key-takeaways-fr

United States antitrust law. (2022, December 14) In Wikipedia. Available at: https://en.wikipedia.org/wiki/United_States_antitrust_law

V-Dem Institute (2022) *India Now an Electoral Autocracy*: Swedish Firm V-Dem Institute, Available at: (https://www.youtube.com/watch?v=o0K_Hg4j-SU), dated March 12, 2021

Wheare, K.C.; en.wikipedia.org › wiki › Kenneth Wheare.

Wikipedia (2022) *Hindu nationalism 2022, November 7*, Available at: https://en.wikipedia.org/wiki/Hindu_nationalism

World Bank (2011) *World Development Report, 2011*, Available at:

https://web.worldbank.org/archive/website01306/web/pdf/wdr2011_full_text.pdf.

You Tube (2019) *Godse and Savarkar, Both Must Be Rejected.* Available at: https://www.youtube.com, dated Nov. 28, 2019.

www.ingramcontent.com/pod-product-compliance
Lightning Source LLC
LaVergne TN
LVHW041606070526
838199LV00052B/3016